The Science of Successful Living

THE SCIENCE OF

Successful Living

BY RAYMOND CHARLES BARKER

DEVORSS *Publications*

ISBN: 0-87516-536-2
Library of Congress Catalog Card: 57-11392

Fifth Printing, 2002

DeVorss & Company, Publisher
P.O. Box 550
Marina del Rey, CA 90294-0550
w w w . d e v o r s s . c o m

Printed in the United States of America

Foreword

FEW PEOPLE think of life as a creative experiment. Most of us are so busy with routines that we take life for granted. We expect an endless routine of work, a hectic social life each weekend and two weeks' vacation each year. I trust that the readers of this book will derive from it a new interest in life, a zest for doing what needs to be done and a technique to live with joyous enthusiasm.

Looking at life from an inspired viewpoint you can see those things which are on the side of greatness and cease resisting the petty and the unimportant. Life is a process of intelligence. It always acts intelligently. Problems are the result of living life unintelligently.

Work with your world the way it works. To drive a car, you have to drive it the way a car should be driven. You can't drive it as you would a locomotive, an airplane or a boat. Life can be lived fully, provided you live it according to the basic patterns of Life itself.

The creative power in life is mind. That is its primary quality and its most basic function. The universe is the result of a mathematical thinker, thinking mathematically. One authority said that the only real difference between matter and mind was that mind is an area of ideas in fluidic form and matter is an area of ideas temporarily locked up in form.

The universe is actually a mental system. Its primary nature is the process of ideas becoming form. Every fact in your world is also an idea in your mind. To get new things in your world you must have new ideas in your consciousness. Few people do enough abstract thinking to create new ideas in their minds. They continually think about what they already know and have known for years. This explains the monotony of their lives.

To increase the area of man's consciousness has been the aim of all religion and education. The infiltration of new ideas in the mind is essential to healthy living. You exist in an infinite Mind which offers you an ever-expanding variety of ideas. Ideas are seeking to be born in your mind.

Select the idea of some new experience you want and then think it without ceasing. Mind will deliver to you everything you need in order to accomplish your demonstration. This is far from being impossible. The great, the wise and the true have proven this to be so. You have done it and so have your friends. You may

not have thought of the process as being either spiritual
or psychological. You intuitively knew a new idea.
Your thinking in terms of this idea caused something
to happen in your experience.

This book has been written for that large section
of today's population which is spiritually liberal and
psychologically aware. Those bound by traditional beliefs will cast it aside. It is my desire that thousands
will be helped and healed by reading these pages.

Contents

The Science of Successful Living

1

The Necessity of Creative Ideas

POWER IS NOT in what you do, what you own nor in the health of your body. Power is in the use of your mind and emotions. Your consciousness determines the way life works for you, for it can only work for you by working through you. Ideas have to use the materials which are within you. These materials are your mental attitudes, your fears, your memory and your desires.

Ever since man began his first primitive groping for a belief in God, and thereby developed religion, his spiritual thinking has revealed to him one central idea. Every religion has taught it and every savior has exemplified it. It is, that belief determines your experience. What you are on the inside determines what you experience on the outside. Your faith in good increases your area of good. Your faith in negatives, which is fear, increases your problems.

There is a science of the mind, a way of handling thought and feeling to get the most out of life. This science does not teach that you can be happy, prosperous and healthy all the time. That would be nonsense. However, this science does teach that you can greatly improve your mental attitudes and as a result you will certainly be happier, healthier and have greater ease in finance. These areas of life are determined by the types of ideas functioning in your consciousness, and you can always improve your ways of thinking and feeling.

Spiritual thinkers have realized the importance of directing the mind to great ideas rather than keeping it at the level of daily routines which absorb you with the petty, the tiresome and the disconcerting. Their advice has been to think of the nature of God, the living spirit within you and of those elements of life which are creative, expanding and eternal. If you have done this you have proven to yourself that this technique works. Fixing your attention on a positive goal causes Life to back you up with all its processes and you realize that the universe is for you and never against you. You live with greater ease and are able to give ease to others.

The Infinite Mind created your consciousness to be a positive, creative, active area of influence. Fears, unhappiness, sickness and lack are a misuse of your mind. It was never designed to work with these vicious and destructive emotions. That is why they wreak their havoc upon you. God knew what He was doing when

He gave you the capacity to think in large terms, to perceive great truths and to experience love in its highest forms. You are divinely equipped to think what the great have thought, through their books, music, art, theatre and science. In addition, your equipment of consciousness includes your ability to have original ideas arise within you.

No man has ever contemplated the Divine Nature of himself and not been benefited. From within comes the urge to select in life that which is greater than you now know. From this same intuitive source comes the whisper of God saying you need not be sick, unhappy, frustrated and struggling with financial problems. Life is an inlet and an outlet, an ebb and a flow. It is something you receive and give. Ideas enter your mind and actions follow. Thoughts come to your mind and you do something about them. If they are negative you worry, fear and doubt. If they are creative, you are inspired to right and loving action.

You are forever immersed in and a part of, a Creative Mind. This Mind is thinking new ideas into your consciousness. Accept them by knowing that they come to you in order to operate through you and bring to pass something greater in your experience than you have had previously. Welcome them as you would a dear friend. Life seeks in every way to inspire your mind. It wants you to have more and more of all good things. It knows no lack, limitation nor impossibility.

God never knows defeat.

There is no virtue in pain, poverty or unhappiness. Unhappiness has never improved a living soul. It cannot increase your area of good, it will only diminish it. It warps, destroys and contracts. The Infinite can only release Its ideas into the consciousness that is at peace with itself and enjoying the experience of living.

Happiness is determined by the ideas working in your consciousness, not by your environment, possessions, social activities or your hopes. Happiness knows no time, it is always a present action. Your mentality is always under your personal control. Your mind always displays itself. It makes itself obvious. As you enter a room people glance at you and know your mood. You give to others only what you are. In my book *Treat Yourself to Life* is this sentence: "Your happiness is in direct ratio to your ability to give yourself to others."

Givingness is the basis of all living. It is the cause of all friendship, love, family life and social activities. However, the boundaries of your mind determine your capacity to give. The ideas that predominate in your thinking are what you share with your world. Greatness offers itself to you. All of love gives of itself in you. Life has never imprisoned anyone. It cannot, by its own nature, limit you. God offers to you Ideas which will make you free from the false conclusions of your own negative thinking. Take them and rejoice.

You are free to take what you want from life and give what you will to life. You are spiritually free, though for the moment you may be materially in bondage. Lack of income may, for the moment, prevent you from doing what you want. Poor health, a sense of duty to family or an obligation to business is a passing experience to those who let in the ideas of God. You are free to think anything you want to think.

If you want to treat yourself to life, place your attention on ideas which will cause you to move ahead. These ideas already dwell in you and await your recognition. God in the midst of you is inspiring you at this moment. Say to yourself:

There is but one mind, one life, one good, God. To me are given the ideas of God, and they now are alive within me. I accept them with joy. I give them their full freedom to operate through me and bring to pass a finer experience for me. I give them all power and authority to accomplish their purpose. I rejoice in them and am glad.

The consistent repetition of ideas is a process of learning. Think back to your school days and you will verify this. In the field of mental attitudes the repetition of ideas is most important. The constant repeti-

tion of negatives in your thinking causes your subconscious mind to produce more difficulties in your
experience. Possibly you dread the future. You can't
see much health, prosperity or happiness ahead of you.
If you will watch your thinking and your moods, you
will discover the reason for this. Over the past months,
perhaps years, you have been mentally convincing
yourself each day that the future is dark. From early
morning until late at night, without realizing it, you
consistently think and speak negatives. Your whole
approach to your work and your recreation is the
expectancy of trouble. Why wouldn't you feel de-
pressed and be certain that others who are successful
have a special claim on heaven?

The Bible teaches that your real inner thinking about
yourself becomes a law to your experience. Such
teaching is as old as the first wise man who ever lived
and appreciated life. The repetition of trouble at the
conscious mind level day after day indicates increased
trouble ahead. Your religion should have taught you
to believe in the goodness of life, its endless oppor-
tunities and your ability to achieve what you want, for
the living Spirit indwells you.

If you are unhappy or in some form of tragedy, you
may not believe this, but when you do believe it, your
problems will begin their dissolution. Why should life
give you anything better than what you now have, if
your thinking remains at a dead level? A chronic in-

valid cannot gain health while his mental attitude maintains the illness. If you are in a chronic financial problem, why should the creative power prosper you, if your constant attention is on how little you have? Life can only give you what you are mentally conditioned to accept. Consistent belief that you haven't what you want will never cause what you want to happen to you.

There is an exactness to life; there is a science of living. The Creative Mind delivers to you the exact results of your states of mind. This is the law of cause and effect. Both Jesus and Paul taught it. You can only have in your world what you are mentally and emotionally conditioned to have. By changing your conditioning through the repetition of spiritual ideas, you change what you receive from life.

The power and wisdom of God have never planned a negative program for anyone. If you dread something in the future, you need a good swift spiritual shot in the arm. You need to treat yourself by contemplating the nature of God and your place and function in His Mind. The Infinite's program for you is a roadway of positives. It must do this for It could not do otherwise, as It knows only good. The more you affirm that you are spiritual and divine, the more good happens to you.

Your mind is a directing center of life. Your mental conclusions are your only limitations. There are no

shut doors and no finalities in this world. To believe
that you are at the end of your road is stupid. The pathway is endless and you are a free agent. The action of
God is not limited to any group, church denomination
or ritual. It is limited only by your capacity to think
in terms of what you want, instead of continuing your
contemplation of what you do not want.

New ideas are the key to new experiences. Saying
that success, true love or perfect health have passed
you by only means that you have let it go past. It
means you did not have a creative mental attitude to
hold it in your experience. You can change every situation in your life for the better once you have decided
to do it and seek a spiritual means of doing it. The
Mind of God is seeking to find those of Its creation
who are willing to release the past, live in the present
with new ideas and plan a creative future for themselves.

In 1932 in the depths of the world depression a
woman came to see me who was almost destitute. She
pled with me to show her a way of changing her consciousness so she could again have prosperity and freedom in money. The only question I asked was "What
is the one thing above all others that you would like to
do?" Her reply was that she had always wanted to be
a pastry specialist. Remember that in 1932 she couldn't
have found a job as a regular baker, let alone a specialist in fancy pastries. In those years such delicacies

were rarely used.

I said to her, "Then go ahead and do it." She looked at me in complete amazement. I said, "If we together subconsciously accept the idea that you can be this, then every door will open for you to do it." She did not argue: she did not say it was impossible; she agreed with me. I gave her the following treatment:

There is no limitation in the Universal Spirit which is God. It remains forever the same. God knows neither depression nor impossibility. You are the vital outlet of Divine Ideas. You now welcome them and rejoice in them. Every limited poverty idea is now erased from your consciousness. To you is given by the Mind of God your right and perfect employment in the field you want. You accept this idea, and the Law of Mind is already in action producing it.

You are free from all fear and established in all faith. God moves you forward into your successful career. Rejoice and be exceeding glad.

Both of us believed her desire to be sound, even though the world at that time would never have called it practical. In ways beyond anything the human mind would have thought possible, a noted manufacturer of flours arranged a one-week pastry school at the Waldorf-Astoria Hotel in New York City. Out of thousands of applicants, she was one of those chosen.

Living four hundred miles from New York, she hitch-hiked to the city. Upon completing the course she was considered so unusual that she was offered a job as a pastry specialist in one of the few wealthy clubs able to survive during the depression. She has been constantly employed in that type of work at the finest clubs and hotels ever since, receiving a large salary.

Not once did she allow herself the luxury of fear, doubt or failure. She held fast to her belief that in right ways her good would come to pass because a Mind larger than her own would cause it to happen. Her constant thought was "There is a Power in me, acting through me, and acting for me which causes me to accomplish what I want." She knew that her mind was the place where the Power acted, and she kept it clear. She projected the idea with authority and allowed no one to discourage her. She realized that controlling her mind and emotions was a full time job and she never wavered for a moment.

What this woman did, you can do. God plays no favorites. His Mind and Law are equally available to all. You can always change conditions, when you decide to do it, and follow through with the necessary disciplines of mind. You are mind in action. Even your body can only do and be what your consciousness decides. Every action and condition of your body is the result of subconscious thought action. Body is a field of response, never one of cause. It reacts, but cannot act of itself. Your sickness or health is the result of your subconscious thinking and you can always change this by introducing a new positive train of causative thinking based on a spiritual idea.

Life is the interaction of ideas. It is the play of thought and feeling upon the great screen of experience. Your combined use of thought and feeling, plus the direction you have given these, makes your life what it is today. And, your use and direction of them determines your future. Consciousness is the cause of all experience. In your hands is the responsibility of living. You are a free agent in a Mind that delivers to you the exact reactions of your mental actions.

Life is spiritual activity. In the commonplace is the Spirit. It exhibits intelligence, purpose and plan. As a living soul, you have intelligence, purpose and plan.

An infinite Wisdom caused you to be born in these times. The Mind of God knew exactly what it was doing when you were born. You are a specialized creation of the Almighty. In you God has individualized His mind, power and authority, so that you could create what you want when you want it. But most people cannot believe this. They have been conditioned by their religion to think of themselves as helpless. They never grasp the reins of life and proceed in the direction they would like to go. Either you act with authority upon your world, or your world will give you an average existence.

here is an Intelligence which arranges many things behind the outer scene, a Mind which knows exactly what to do, when to do it, and proceeds to fulfill your ideas. God is tremendous, magnificent and creative and all of It is yours. The more you rejoice in being a part of It, the more Life can enrich and benefit you. Say to yourself:

I rejoice in life. I rejoice in these times in which I live. I behold the goodness and the richness of life on every hand. I am the full Mind and Love of God in complete expression right now. I find so much in my life that is good. I know my victory over problems is certain for I know that my intelligence is a part of God.

Remember this at the end of a hard and busy day. Your fatigue is natural. You have faced and met problems. You have handled things to the best of your ability. That is all that Life requires of anyone. So be glad to be alive in these days right where you are. If you don't like your present routines, you can change them. There is never despair to one who knows this science. He senses the divinity within humanity and the answer within the question. Problems become exciting experiments, and faith is never dimmed.

There is no simple rule for a happier life. Successful living is hard work, but this hard work is simplified when you realize it takes place in your consciousness.

Life is the movement of intelligence through law an
order producing what you select to have in your experience. I realize that you cannot keep your mind
affirmative twenty-four hours a day. No individual can
do this. However, you can take five minutes each morning to quietly and confidently do spiritual thinking.
Contemplate spiritual ideas and believe them possible
for you to demonstrate. You have a right to health,
peace of mind, a goodly measure of this world's goods
and creative self-expression.

In your time of dedication to Truth, know that your
life right now is a part of God and contains all the
possibilities of full and rich living. Accept yourself as
an intelligent loving expression of life. Do not think
of your mistakes and failures during this period. They
are unimportant to the Divine Wisdom. It knows them
not and is not interested in what you might have done.
God is only interested in what you are and where you
have chosen to go. You are the image and likeness of
the creative power. You are an expanding, unfolding
consciousness backed up by the universal Mind. God
wants you to be what you want to be. In your quiet
thinking select your future, then accept it as normal
for you, and then expect it to happen. Give thanks that
all the ways and means to bring it to pass are already
in action. Rest in the calm assurance that the Intelligence of God is making all things possible.

The above is self-treatment. It is establishing cause

and the Law of Being will produce the effect. With this new concept firmly implanted in your mind things begin to happen. Follow through by letting changes come. Don't expect things to remain as they are. This they cannot do, for you have set in motion a powerful idea which acts with exactness in creating a new experience.

2

The Operative Action of Mind

MAN IS THE enigma of the universe. Despite the sciences developed to define him, he remains only partially understood. Medicine, anatomy, physiology and psychology only explain how he works but they cannot behold the inner man of the spirit which is why he is. The experiments at Duke University in the department of Parapsychology, under the direction of Dr. J. B. Rhine, have come the nearest to understanding the indwelling spirit.

Organized religion has insisted upon the degradation of the individual. This premise was necessary for their purposes, but it has held the bulk of people in a false bondage for thousands of years. An impartial reading of the four biographies of Jesus, the four gospels, makes you wonder at the doctrines perpetuated in his name. In many churches there has been a response to the idea that man needs salvation because he sought a reason outside himself for his failures.

The word sin is intriguing. The child likes to be thought of as naughty and the adult likes to think he often can be beyond convention. It is an ego builder. Take the emphasis on sin and degradation out of most religious doctrines and you have little left. Thousands are awakening to a larger concept of God and a greater concept of Man. The growth of the metaphysical groups and churches in the last fifty years is amazing to behold.

The natural man is a spiritual potential. Left alone he will not go to his doom but will progress, evolve rapidly and bring forth a better world than he ever knew before. Man is essentially good. The evil characteristics of the human mind and emotions are merely the left-overs from his trail of evolution. They are bad habits we have not yet handled rightly as we have grown tall in the ways of the mind and the spirit. Along the road of evolution you have gradually learned the ways of life and have accumulated wisdom. Within you, right now, is the accumulated wisdom of the ages. It awaits your recognition and upon your recognition it reveals the full area of its knowledge.

As people we are far from perfect, but we are well along our way. Looking back to primitive man we can see how far we have come. Noting this we should not fear the future. Those who say that man is inherently a sinner, inherently negative and inherently evil can point out the flaws which are apparent in each of us.

They are obvious to the husband, the wife, the child and especially obvious to the trained psychologist, social worker, clergyman or metaphysician.

It is easy to sit back in life and realize why we aren't where we ought to be. Such speculation on the past is psychologically and metaphysically vicious, as it keeps the mind's attention on evil rather than on planning a good. No one ever is improved by your telling him his faults. You have learned this from experience. Self-improvement cannot be forced on anyone. Unless it arises as a desire within the individual, it never will accomplish its purpose. The age of trying to reform people is gone. Modern psychology has awakened us to the fact that information heals but reformation only increases guilt.

The need for praise and recognition is inherent in man. You respond to praise as much as you cringe under condemnation. I account for the endurance, continuity and prosperity of the Jews, despite the fact that no other single group in all history has endured so much misunderstanding, by the fact that the principle of praise was the basis of their religious beliefs. As you read the Old Testament you realize this to be so. The name Judah means praise in the original Hebrew. Though their praising was to an external God, nevertheless, it sustained their vitality and endurance through their many vicissitudes.

Jesus taught praise as one of his main ideas. He

knew the healing therapy of it. Praise is a balm to the soul and a boon to the heart. About the only place you can find joyous praise today is in the Pentecostal or Fundamentalist churches. It is interesting that the two religious groups showing the greatest increase in active numbers in the last twenty years have been the Fundamentalists and the Metaphysicians. In both groups, the recognition of God is paramount and the expectation that God will do wonderful things here and now is emphasized.

By describing your troubles you do not heal them. Pointing out to yourself the places where you do not measure up never will improve you. Self-depreciation is a vicious misuse of the human mind. The greatest single problem in man today, psychologically, is his sense of guilt. Every psychologist, psychiatrist and psycho-analyst will agree with me on that statement. Any religion which increases your guilt sense is harmful, for it increases the guilt load in your subconscious mind.

The next time a friend says to you across a luncheon table, "There is something I think you should know," reply quickly, "I don't want to hear it." It only will make you feel uneasy and unhappy. It will create in you no desire to improve. Only praise and appreciation make you want to go ahead to greater things. You know well enough your errors of omission and commission. When you are really ready to do something about them, you will. Until that time, all discussion is useless and it only makes you feel more guilty.

The years before you with their possibilities are far more important than sitting in judgement on yourself for past and present errors. You can grow in wisdom and the right handling of life by the normal process of evolution which will take untold millions of years, or you can decide right now to devote more time to considering the Spirit within you, and through right thinking speed up the process. On the pathway of improvement, you do not keep your attention on where you are but on where you are going. There is at the center of you an impulsion to greatness. Direct all your efforts to expansion and you will be led into greater good.

You live in the outpictured experience of your own mentality. Your present world is the result of the sum total of your beliefs about life. You cannot dodge the responsibilities of growth and maturity. Those who try it find themselves in painful and destructive situations. The universe does not tolerate lawlessness. It knows only cause and effect. Your thinking takes place in a law of mind action, which produces scientifically and accurately your consciousness into form. Around you is your thought in form. Good or bad, this still is true.

The universe responds to you as you respond to it. It has never forced anything upon you. Everything that has happened to you was the result of a conscious or subconscious receptivity on your part. Life flows acng to law. Life gravitates to the point where you are in the ways of your mind. A teacher of these ideas years ago developed the following cliche, "You are where you are, because of what you are, and you are what you are, because of what you consistently believe."

That is a truth. Jesus said it in the words, "As thou hast believed, so be it done unto thee." (Matthew 8:13) Life adjusts to your patterns. It particularly creates according to your own self-acceptance. What you really believe you are gives direction to life. It is psychologically impossible to maintain sanity without self-acceptance. Spiritually, it is a necessity to see yourself as an inlet and an outlet of the Creative Power and to act as though it were so, for it is so.

You have unconsciously accepted yourself, you have come to terms with yourself. Your judgement may not be known to you, but it is so. This inner appraisal causes your life to be what it is. Life can only press upon your shoulders what you have predetermined by your own mental and emotional conditioning. Those who attempt to fight back at life have a losing battle. They are fighting effect, not cause. They are actually fighting their own minds and don't realize it. The immensity of God indwells you. You can trust Its ways and means. But it only can bring to pass the decisions of your thinking, not your hopes, your visions nor your aspirations. It produces for you what you first induce in consciousness.

You are God at the self-conscious level of mind action. The Infinite cannot act through any other form of life consciously as it does in man. In all lesser forms of life It acts subconsciously. Only man is a conscious expression of intelligence having volition to carve out his own destiny. This capacity within you is the spirit of the living God. Paul called it "Christ in you, the hope of glory." (Colossians 1:27) Jesus spoke of it as "the Father in me." (John 14:10) In metaphysics it is the Divine Idea or the Divine Pattern of man.

In you is that which is born "not of the blood, nor of the will of the flesh, nor of the will of man, but of God." (John 1:13) This inner Spirit, Mind and Power knows neither limitation, time nor space. It only knows that you are Its embodiment. It is a realm of pure ideas, unlimited right action and completed results. It sees all things finished from the beginning. It knows you as the triumphant man. God in you, as you, is the undefeated possibility of all that you can be. As you think of yourself in these terms, you begin to live effectually and with a minimum of confusion. You see the road ahead as being good and you rejoice that you are traveling under divine direction. Say to yourself:

I rejoice in that Life which lives by means of me.
I am the incarnation of the whole Spirit of life.
Christ in me is my hope of glory. I let the uncon-

*tioned Mind of God be in me all that It seeks to
be. I accept victory. I never am afraid, for I know
the Divine Presence within is my sure salvation.*

Life is the most complicated, yet orderly process
ever devised by the Intelligence of God. Life is rarely
easy but with right mental attitudes it can be a creative
and adventurous experience. As you acknowledge your
life to be the action of God, it impels you toward
greatness. You move from where you are to where you
want to be. Defining yourself as a human being in a
material world, eking out a dull existence is an insult
to the Divine which fashioned you. It is an incomplete
picture. It is as though you went to a symphony con-
cert and heard only the string instruments and failed
to hear the others. You would say the music was
valueless. The full symphony of your real self only can
be heard when all the windows of your mind are open
to the fullness of life. Only when body, home, work
and income are seen as phases of a larger picture does
life reveal its full horizon to your awareness. Fortunately, more people in each generation are realizing
that life without spiritual understanding cannot portray
the full man. A new appraisal of man is taking place
and that is a healthy indication.

Many people have hope and aspiration without a
working technique to make them effective. When you
are ill the doctor establishes you in a definite regime to

allow the latent health in you to be restored. He prescribes rest, right diet, freedom from anxiety, and order in general. For years you have known you needed these factors in balance in your living, but you neglected them. Hope and aspiration remain as pleasant dreams until you arrange your patterns to do something specific about them.

When you really want to go, where you now think you would like to go, you will set up a regime of thought, feeling and action to get there. Until such a time your discussions about what you would like to do or be are useless. When you want to improve, you will. Until that time arrives, there is little to be done about it. Life has equipped you with intelligence and emotion. It offers you every opportunity in the world. You can select what you want. Once you have selected what you want with determination the power moves into action through you, and the way unfolds. This power within knows no defeat. It knows only growth, expansion and unfoldment of ideas into definite form. You are the living representative of an unconditioned Mind, which is always thinking of you as being unconditioned. Link your thinking with the thoughts of God and no man, situation nor world condition can stop your becoming what you have selected to become.

Jesus could have remained a carpenter in a small village in Galilee and lived in moderate comfort all his life. Moses could have been a quiet shepherd on the plains of Midian and never worried about the Hebrew slaves in Egypt. Every great man or woman on the face of the globe who has ever moved forward in the evolution of his own soul, has done so because he wanted to do so, plus devising a plan for doing it. Greatness is not inherited, it is fashioned out of the thought and feeling of the individual.

Spiritual evolution is yours for the taking. It requires your decision, your willingness to let go of present comfort and launch out into paths of new trials with their inevitable good results. To do this you cease from condemning your human mind and its mistakes. Start to see yourself as God's representative on earth. The whole creative process is in your mind and heart awaiting your acknowledgement.

Where you are in the world of cold facts is an indication of where you are in consciousness. Experience is in direct ratio to belief. Where you will go in the coming year will be determined by what you believe about yourself. To progress in any area, you have to think in larger terms. Jesus selected what he wanted life to do for him, and defined the inner creative action which would bring the results to pass. "The Father that dwelleth in me, He doeth the works." (John 14:10) Jesus decided whom to heal and the Power healed. He decided whom to feed, and the Power did the rest of the work. Select where you want to go and the Power immediately acts to get you there.

Birth is always taking place where you are. Something forever is being born into form, and other things are dying out of form. This is the endless play of life upon itself. What you mentally and emotionally release dies out of your world. What you mentally and emotionally embody is born into your world. Not only select what you want in life, but select also those things you no longer want. Let them die. They will move out of your experience if you refuse to sustain them with your attention. The old order has to pass away to let God create what you want. The clutter of the present has to be streamlined to allow the future to take place.

In every point in space, in every instant of time and in every atom of matter birth is taking place. New ideas are appearing, new attitudes are available and new hopes appear on the horizons of your thinking. Only your negatives prevent this spiritual action from refashioning your world. Negatives are the guideposts to detours for the creative process. They are the labyrinth in which the divine power is lost. You know intuitively those factors in your consciousness which are holding you back. Declare their death in your thinking and be free of them. Destroy them with deliberate intent. They are road blocks which should not be. Divine Intelligence needs your full cooperation to bring to pass your heart's desires. You give it freedom to act by affirming what you want and denying the subconscious patterns which say you cannot have it.

Say to yourself:

*God is where I am and a phase of God is what
I want.*

Money, right work, peace of mind, health, love and
creative self-expression are normal and natural phases
of the Spirit. They are intended for you. The divine plan
includes them and the equipment to produce them already is yours. Your present mind is an operating center
for the creative spirit. It only needs to be cleansed of the
beliefs in impossibility to make the impossible possible.
Spirit is your conscious mind thinking capacity. You
did not originate this, nor can you cause it to cease. You
can direct it only. Every thought is a creative force, a
creative movement in mind. It has power and authority.
It executes itself. Your conscious mind is the most valuable asset you have. You probably take the least care
of it and do not watch the directions it is giving at
every instant to your subconscious. You think anything you want to think, good, negative or unimportant. Months or years later you wonder why certain
unpleasant situations happen. If you know mental science the explanation is simple. Your conscious mind
is cause. Discipline cause and you will have a disci-
plined effect. Things don't happen, they are caused.
Problems do not come upon you, you create them.

Knowing this you have a pathway to freedom. Say yourself:

I accept the responsibility of life. I now dedicate my thinking to that which I want to be and to have. I know that I can have all the good I can vision. I now destroy out of my subconscious mind every negative block which prevents my demonstration. These are no more. God's action in me is now complete, and I progress with right thinking. I expect results and I give thanks now for these results.

Everyone operates at his own level of consciousness. Actually, every person you know is doing the best he can with the mental attitudes and the fixed opinions which dominate his mind. I have learned not to condemn anyone I know, for his present state of consciousness causes him to be what he is. True, I wish he didn't do what he does, but I have learned to mind my own business. My friends can only evolve through their own self choosing. I have no condemnation. I understand that my good is not dependent upon other people, it is dependent upon my present attitude.

Consciousness changes momentarily. Your present convictions can change in an instant. Any major situation can be changed if you will change. The wise man blames no one. He looks within himself and perceives the cause which is operating and changes it to the causes he wishes to experience. He knows that the arena of his mind must have been caught in the throes of the negative. He then thinks of God, the eternal Good, the source of new viewpoints and lets fresh thinking appear and different conditions prevail.

Religion says that within you is a center of pure goodness. The most depraved individual has this inner spirit. In him, it is a source of irritation for it beckons him intuitively toward the better. God in the midst of you is right intention, clear in its motives and urging you to act with integrity. This inner urge of the Spirit says, "Follow thou me." Moving in God's direction you use greater wisdom, clearer thinking and you seek to love more greatly. The world hungers for the man who thinks in large terms, acts with integrity and produces through love those things which increase his stature in God and blesses and benefits his fellowman.

Power is where you are in what you think. Love awaits your distribution of it. There are no hindrances to self-advancement save those which abide in you, through your own wrong acceptances. God wants you to be what you want to be.

3

God and Your Subconscious

THE SUBCONSCIOUS mind was discovered by Anton Franz Mesmer and explored and explained by Sigmund Freud. Its creative aspects are used by the metaphysician to create what he wants out of life. This phase of mind is the basis of all types of psychotherapy and spiritual healing. Unknown until the eighteenth century and undefined until the nineteenth, its understanding has caused a complete new appraisal of man. Investigating it revealed that man was predominately a mental and emotional individual, not just a body creature. It made evident that man was consciousness and not merely a refined animal.

These revelations should have produced great changes in every religious doctrine, but they didn't. The older religious bodies premised their doctrines on the fact that man was primarily body. Morality was based on what he did or did not do with his body. Religion considered a man virtuous who obeyed the letter of the Ten Commandments. In other words, if he did not kill, commit adultery, swear or get drunk too often, he could be a passable Christian. Orthodoxy inferred that man's body and its desires were the source of his trouble. Man has been told not to sin, meaning not to do some evil physically.

Mesmer, Freud and the modern metaphysician had hoped that this out-moded premise would decline. As it didn't because tradition held fast, a new religion had to be born in which the full understanding of the subconscious as the creative power of the individual could be taught right directions. Emerson prophesied this new religion, which first made its appearance in the 1800s and increased in its following as the years passed. Every major city in the world has churches and groups based on the teaching that the subconscious is the creative power and that man can direct it to make any changes in his life that he wants.

Jesus, 1900 years ahead of his time, taught that the individual was mind in action and that the body could not do wrong, unless the mind was negative. He said that a man who looked upon a woman with adulterous thoughts was as immoral as the man who actually committed the act. He constantly taught belief and faith as the operating functions of experience, and these are mental actions. He advised right thinking, great forgiving, and wise loving. These you do in the mind, not in the body.

Consciousness determines body. Jesus speaking of his body said he could lay it down or pick it up, implying that of itself it had no creative power. Your body and its needs cannot cause you to do a wrong. You must first mentally decide on a course of action and your body fulfills the decision in acts. You must consciously or subconsciously want to do wrong in order for the body to complete the process. An understanding of the conscious and subconscious areas of mind as spiritual, creative processes is the premise of the new religion appearing everywhere today.

Your subconscious mind is the major creative operation in your life. You are ninety percent subconscious in the way you handle life. Everything you do is accomplished by the work of the subconscious. The interaction of the conscious mind (volition) and the subconscious mind (the Law of Action) explain and determine your experience. What you decide with the conscious mind (the Law of Action) explains, and determines, your experience. What you decide with the scious takes the accumulated decisions of your years of living and produces an experience like unto them. It then produces under a law of averages.

There are too many average people, who let this law of averages operate them. Life requires decision as well as desire. Unless you exercise the spiritual gifts of desire plus decision, you will remain an ineffective person. You may be honest, kindly and hard working, only when you give specific direction to your sub-conscious do you become a vital, creative outlet of the Mind of God. The sum-total of all that you have ever thought, felt or experienced is in your subconscious. It resides there not merely as passive memory but also as directive power. All thinking and feeling moves from the level of the conscious to the subconscious where it continues to exist as an influencing power. Unless your conscious mind is motivated by spiritual thinking and high ideals, it will continue to feed the subcon-scious average impressions which will continue in your experience only average results.

A spiritual idea deliberately accepted by the con-scious mind becomes a law of action at the subcon-scious level. Spiritual thinking is a command to the subconscious to produce a good. This command the subconscious must accept and fulfill. It never can negate a spiritually authorized idea. The spiritual ac-ceptance of health consciously determined will cause the subconscious to heal the body. The same thing is true in all other areas of life. It is lack of spiritual direc-tion of the subconscious that causes disease and cor-rect direction that maintains health. That is why your health, happiness, peace of mind and prosperity are always under your control, provided you take such control.

As you deliberately think in terms of God, no mat-ter what vocabulary you may use, your thought is a law of creative action. Man has always prayed to his God. Until now he prayed without knowing whether he had a conscious or subconscious mind. He knew only that as he prayed he felt better and improved conditions usually followed. Today, with our clearer understanding of the operation of mind at two levels and their interaction, we can define a science of prayer, and this science we name treatment. Treatment to the metaphysician is a conscious mind selection of a spiritual idea, or prototype, which then is subjectified and becomes a law of mind action which must bring to pass an experience like unto the idea accepted.

Life is made up of two factors—thought and feeling. Philosophers and theologians have taught duality. But, their duality was one of good and evil, light and darkness, right and wrong. Today, with our new understanding of the conscious and the subconscious, we see that duality is ended when the unity of the two phases of mind is understood and right directions are given to them for right living. You are spirit and soul. Your conscious mind is spirit; your subconscious is soul.

When the Spirit of God enters the soul of man he is redeemed out of all creeds, all wrong beliefs and all problems. As your conscious mind chooses a creative idea, a God idea, and delivers It to your subconscious, the Law of Mind makes glad your experience. What people called prayer was this process. They didn't know it by that name, but intuitively they practiced it.

We call it treatment for it indicates an action on your part to correct your own states of consciousness. Prayer has now moved from the nebulous to the scientific.

Knowing an omnipresent God, you have no one to whom to pray. Gone are all personality, whims and caprice, clouds, thrones and golden streets. That is why some people find it difficult to feel at home in this teaching. Their training has been such that a personal God is necessary to them. They still need the feeling that God will do something for them because of their religious belief that he might not do for others. To say that God is everywhere evenly present means to many that God is nowhere. But this step has to be taken if you want to practice scientific Christianity.

The Creative Mind is everywhere evenly distributed and acts through all creation with even purpose and intent. There is no more of God where I am than where you are. All of God is equally present at every point in space, and in each person regardless of his particular religious conviction. In you, the Divine Intelligence knows what to do, and proceeds to do it, if It has the cooperation of the two areas of your thinking. Your mental attitudes determine the effectiveness of the Spirit in your world. The Lord God Omnipotent reigns, but only the wise in mind let that perfect action be in them. They do this by using their minds aright.

The evolution of man indicates purpose. The power

which has brought us this far according to an intelligent plan will take us the rest of the way. However, it seeks our cooperation. This cooperation we can give if we use our minds, for the apparent reason that they were created. Looking at life on a broad scale we are amazed at the pettiness of most human thinking. We see the misuse and misdirection of the conscious and subconscious bringing to pass the minor, while all the time the major is available and possible.

To spend the greatest amount of your time each week earning and spending money, washing, clothing and feeding the body with a few additional hours of recreation will never induce spiritual evolution. These things need to be done, but your mental attitude while doing them determines whether you are on the pathway of the Spirit, or merely putting in the necessary years from the date on your birth certificate until finally there is a date on your death certificate.

Your moods are determined by your subconscious mind. The sum total of your previous experience and feelings usually determines them. However, at any moment that you choose, the conscious mind can alter and improve the moods and tones of life set by the subconscious. Creative ideas can never make their appearance through unhappy states of mind. Sorrow, bitterness, depression and like attitudes are blocks in the pathway of creative living. Lingering in these moods you bring destruction into your experience, for you are giving false directions to your subconscious. You are using it in a way for which it was never devised.

God made man to be creative; to bring to pass through his conscious intelligence, acting on his subconscious law of mind action, great new experiences. We use such a small area of our potentials. Physically, few people breathe deeply enough to use more than a third of the lungs. Only a scattering of people use the full flexibility of their bodies. Too much time is spent hurriedly to accomplish the unimportant, while the vistas of greatness await our outward look and our upward reach.

The creative Mind distributes Itself equally in all Its creations. If any man is an outlet for the Infinite Ideas, then you are. Life shows no partiality. The genius of an Einstein is in every man. The lack of use of man's spiritually endowed genius is shocking to anyone who knows what man can be. It is time to cease being content with the average, and with deliberate intent choose creative ideas and hold them close to you until they are subconsciously established and the law of mind brings them into fruition.

Everything necessary for a creative, dynamic, successful life on this planet you already have. No man who has ever lived has had more mind and emotion than you have. The excuses of lack of opportunity,etc., mean nothing, for today you can always change your thinking, give your subconscious new directions and thereby have a new heaven and a new earth appear as your experience. Your endowment by God is a permanent one. Neither past nor present tragedies, hurts nor patterns of neurosis from childhood have touched the inner Spiritual Reserve of right mind action. Man can be limited by himself, but God in man cannot be limited by man. Say to yourself:

I now dedicate my whole area of mind to the Divine Purpose of creative living. I refuse to be an average person with mediocre results in life. God placed within me the genius of the Spirit. I am no longer in bondage to the past either mentally nor emotionally. Every limited pattern in my subconscious mind is now obliterated by this treatment, which is the word of God. I consciously think new and greater ideas, and these now subconsciously are the cornerstone of my thinking. Therefore, through the action of God in me there now appears in my world increased good in every form.

Select a new project to accomplish in the next few months. The idea of it is where you are and already in your consciousness. It seeks you and needs you for its manifestation. As you think in its terms expect it to come to pass. Refuse all negative mental speculation that it cannot happen. Believe that the Divine Wisdom wants you to have this new experience and act as though it were a fact. Don't listen to others' doubts, and keep clear of your own. Doing this you will make your demonstration.

It is a spiritual necessity to maintain a creative state of consciousness. One day we shall know from the psychologists how much of the body deterioration which takes place after the age of fifty is due to the mind accepting the belief that it can no longer create. The study of geriatrics and psychosomatic medicine may eventually reveal that as our minds cease being creative the body ceases in direct ratio from a vital one into one of endurance and gradual disintegration. Usually, where you find a creative mind you find a creative body. A stimulated mind generates a stimulated atmosphere and a stimulated environment. Such a person surrounds himself with creative, stimulating people. They gather together just as the lonely, the sick and the complaining gather together. Take a look at your friends and behold your mind outpictured.

Every creative person sets up vital currents in life that enrich the world. He has subconsciously accepted life as a vital, joyous experience and his consciousness seeks out the unusual. He wants fresh ideas in his mind. He chooses to keep his world flexible and his viewpoints expanding. He is clear in his certainty of good. He expects the good and gives the good. The entire area of both his conscious and subconscious minds is alive with the present and creatively anticipating the future.

He is living life as the Divine Mind intended it should be lived.

If you consciously work with the ideas that the Infinite is impelling in your consciousness, your subconscious mind has to accept them and act upon them. The subconscious cannot refuse any idea, mood nor demand upon it. Being impersonal, it doesn't know what you are delivering to it in your everyday thinking. It knows only how to produce according to the materials given it. It is a doer not a knower. It is a productive field but does not know what it is producing.

It is as easy to demonstrate a creative life as it is a dull one. The same mental equipment is used for either. The contemplation of problems destroys creativity. The intelligent search for solutions increases the creative capacity of your mind. There always is more power in good than in evil. If this weren't so the world would long ago have been overcome with evil. But, today good is still the greatest commodity in life and love has more victory than hate. You cannot afford to let your problems ruin your creative thinking. Worry is a false luxury that creates damage at the subconscious level. It is the introduction into the creative process of a factor which must by its very nature disrupt the creative flow of constructive living. Fear, worry and deep anxiety are to the metaphysician what the devil is to the usual church goers.

The devil is nothing more or less than the human

mind believing a lie. To believe that your troubles are beyond solution is a lie. This belief gives authority to the subconscious to continue the problem and intensify it. This mis-direction of consciousness is blasphemy. God created you and gave you your mental equipment to bring forth creative experiences, and your acceptance of evil in any form is an insult to the Intelligence that fashioned you out of Itself.

Life is the only real power, and this power is one of consciousness. When your consciousness accepts a negative as normal, you are giving a vicious authority to your subconscious to create. There is authority in disease. When a friend is ill, watch that authority work in his consciousness. His acceptance of it gives the disease free reign in his mind and body. The negative intelligence in the disease-idea knows exactly how to proceed to fulfill its destructive work. It creates its damage with amazing ease. Yet, it functions only because it has been given acceptance and subconscious authority to function.

When you cease authorizing negatives by your depth belief in them, they will occur no more in your world. The only evil power there is, is your human mind when it is convinced that you are limited by the conditions of your experience. The saints are those who have searched themselves and baptized their own thinking until it is crystal-clear, and they can be confounded no more. These are the people who have laid the groundwork for all men's greatness to appear. They have said to life, "I can and I will." They have remained steadfast in their sure knowing that Good alone is true and Love alone is the answer.

There are two ways of directing your subconscious and you are free to use either. You can use it humanly or divinely. It responds to both and fulfills the commands of both. The human mind use of it wears you out. The spiritual recognition of your subconscious as a divine instrument which produces for you ideas of freedom and your loving right use of them gives you the equivalent of heaven on earth. Then you are in the world but not of it. You live with ease, for you know your Source and hold fast to creative thinking.

It is sad to see the millions who are fooled by material thinking. Their aims are so temporary and their gains so meagre. They have material security accompanied by spiritual poverty. They are possessed by their possessions and in bondage to their way of life. They go to church to be respectable. Their religious beliefs are conventional, traditional and without any energizing power. They need their god only for weddings, funerals and baptisms. They have convinced themselves of their content.

Unless your outer world is balanced by an inner creative world of constructive mind action, you will be so busy with things that you will neglect ideas. You will be so busy doing that you will have no time for being. Things wear out, bodies grow feeble, but the living vital ideas of Truth restore the years that the locusts of material thinking have eaten. In quiet clear knowing of the good is the true strength of man. Those who have sought God have always found His Presence within them. If you will do this, you will prosper in all your ways.

You cannot withdraw from life. The way of the hermit, the religious recluse or fanatic is as much out of balance as the materially dominated individual. If you dodge the affairs of the world hoping thereby to develop spiritual consciousness, you are in for a surprise. Alone on a mountain top, cloistered in a monastery or a convent, you still will have to meet yourself, for you are always your own problem. The present world and its affairs is not negative and from it you should not flee. Where you are the Power of life is. Escape life you cannot, but live it with peace and right motive you can. God beckons to you in the commonplace as well as in the cathedral.

You are alive because the Divine Intelligence needs you as a vehicle of Its own greatness. Flowing with the Divine Pattern you give creative ideas to your subconscious and have your heaven where you are. Your work is easy and your burdens are light. You accomplish with little effort and no strain, for your subconscious is freed of conflict and your goals are certain to you and to the creative process which brings them to completion. You then take your right place in the scheme of things as a co-worker and co-creator with the Divine.

God is an economic Mind. It never creates inane things, for It never knows stupid ideas. In the Divine Economy all things are in their right place, doing their right work for the good of the whole. Therefore, when you take conscious control of your thinking and handle states of consciousness with the same wisdom that you do your money, you are in your right place being an open outlet of the Divine Mind. Then there is no limit to the good and the fine in your life. You are weighed in the balances and not found wanting.

God loves a creative man. Your right use of mind makes you beloved of God and respected by man. The subconscious mind is your friend. Do not fear it. Do not believe the negatives which the world has placed within it. Consciously knowing Truth, you subconsciously embody It and demonstrate It. This is life lived from the highest viewpoint. This is the high plateau whereon you join the great, the wise and the true. Free from the delusion of evil, you live in the consciousness of God.

Each day bears watching. Your moods need your scrutiny. Your ideas should be selected as wisely as you would choose a diamond. When dedicated clear thinking is engendered in the subconscious, you are the fulfilled man. You are the spiritual pioneer for those who have not yet found this path.

4

Resentment Is Ruin

RESENTMENT IS an abnormal direction of emotion
with an unconscious intent of self-destruction. Its in-
dulgence creates havoc in every area of your life. It is
harmful to the body, your business, your friendships
and your finances. Its insidious operation infiltrates
all your unconscious actions. When you allow your
subconscious mind to be saturated with this emotional
malignancy, you are not only in trouble, you are
headed for even more trouble.

The natural and normal state of your emotions is
one of order, peace and givingness or love. God
equipped you to feel the greatness of life and to im-
part your feelings to others. Your emotions are divine
gifts that should always be used rightly. Most people
make no attempt to control their emotions through
understanding their nature and purpose. In fact, most
people are led around by their emotions like sheep
follow a shepherd. It doesn't enter their thinking to

direct them aright.

Man is an emotional being. His emotional structure is a way in which he experiences life and enjoys his experience. Your emotions never were intended to be used destructively. Watch the toll that anger, resentment, jealousy and other negative feeling take out of you. Wrong use of emotion causes depletion and destruction, while their right use is power and enjoyment. The Mind of God is the source of man's thinking nature and the Love of God is the source of his feeling nature. Thinking is masculine and feeling is feminine. Combined they make your total consciousness, which is the real nature of your being.

Your basic drive is one of self-expression. This is so, because the Infinite is seeking self-expression by means of you. It is a necessity of your psychological nature that you express upon life your mental and emotional states. In fact, it is so absolutely essential that you cannot prevent this action from taking place. If you fail to give it a creative outlet through everyday activity, loved ones, friends and your social life, it goes underground in your subconscious with destructive power. Resentment is one of the ways it finds for self-expression when normal means are not provided by your conscious mind.

There is a Spiritual impulse in every person. Your mental and emotional capacities developed in a completely constructive way would create for you a perfect order, a heaven on earth. Unfortunately, no one is able to blend his mind and emotions perfectly due to the stresses and strains of life, particularly in early years. As a metaphysician, you know these two creative fields to be spiritual in nature, and therefore they can be cured of the twistings and warpings which have accumulated through the years.

You are equipped to live healthily in a healthy society. Unfortunately, history has never provided you with a healthy society in which to prove this true. The world stresses have been great in every age. More money will not create peace. Distribution of food to millions who would otherwise starve has been cnly partially effective. A full stomach does not guarantee right thinking. So, you have to work with the world in which you are, and do the best you can to be a right-minded out-going person.

One thing is certain. The world in which you function can limit you only to the extent that you are unable to prevent its conditioning. If you are a person whose emotional life is as near normal as possible, you are able to act upon your world as you like. The aim of correct spiritual instruction is to make you as near normal as possible. That is why most religious systems have included in their therapy some form of confession. The therapeutic value of this is perhaps the greatest single asset the older churches have. To be rid of your guilt feelings is of the greatest importance, for guilt mis-channels the emotions into anxiety.

You can be your own confessor, if you are willing to face frankly the facts of your own making. This is not a pleasant task, but a most valuable one. If you are able to see in a mirror the person you really are and not the person you are trying to be, you are as close to being normal in your mental and emotional life as is possible. Few can do this. Too many hold the mask of their ego before the mirror and see only the injustices that are being perpetuated upon them. They refuse to see what they themselves are doing with life.

Circumstances beyond your normal control may place you in a situation that seemingly defeats you both mentally and emotionally, but with this understanding you need not remain in that predicament. You are not the victim of circumstance, heredity nor environment. Too many people have used these as excuses for accepting defeat. Others with every possible condition set against them have come through victorious. You are in a universe of subconscious intelligence that must respond to your conscious demand upon it. You are a thinking and feeling center in a universal field of mind and emotion. You can always produce new streams of consciousness.

Jesus believed ideas which the people of his day considered impractical and impossible. His thinking, loving nature was based on a normal use of his capacities and the results have changed the world. He did not believe what people thought he should believe. What he believed, he believed with such intensity that the world changed to fit his beliefs. It will do the same for you, if you will believe what you want with an equal intensity. The demonstration of these principles is not for the casually-minded person. Readers of this book may be inspired to change their thinking and emotional patterns for a few days. That will not accomplish results. It is the steadfast day after day right thinking which produces results.

Emotional problems are usually created by personal relationships. As long as you live, you will have to live with people. At the present time, the scientists are developing cures for most diseases, increasing the safety of childbirth and adding fifteen years to the normal life span. This means that there will be an ever-increasing number of people on this planet and you will be among them and having to deal with them. You cannot escape personal relationships. Each year the streets, elevators and apartment houses will be jammed with more people. Not all of them will be your kind of people. Some will annoy you and a few will hurt you. Your relationships with many will be unimportant, but once in a while there will be a person in your life whom you will resent.

What can you do to stop resenting people whose words and actions disturb you? You are in a universe of free will. If you will take the necessary steps to understand the problem, you can stop resentment. The salvation of the world is not locked in a theology. It rests in the fact that any human being can change for the better. This is the whole teaching of the Bible. It most certainly is the instruction of every Messiah. Any religion, any line of thought, philosophical, psychological or metaphysical, which makes you a better and more outgoing person is your religious science.

You may not wish to change your patterns. You may want to continue your resentments because they justify your failure to use your emotions rightly. Yet, deep within everyone is the knowing that such feelings are unjust, unkind and useless. The resentful person is still in the emotional kindergarten. People are the way that life designed them, plus the way that they have used their powers. If you have wisdom, you realize you can change no one. They are what they are, because of the constituency of their mental-emotional patterns. As you cannot change them, you can only change your reactions to them.

No one is evil, and no one means to be vicious. The person you resent is doing the best that he can with the materials he has. If when he comes into your presence you cringe, stop and realize what you are facing. You are facing your own reaction, not his. You are facing an apparently uncontrolable emotional reaction that is subconsciously induced. In other words you are facing a phase of yourself. Often, it is not the person nor the remark that causes the resentment, it is the result of memory. In the past other people, situations and remarks made so deep an impression in your subconscious, that the present person merely out-pictures to you the sum total of the past hurts and you place the blame on him. And, it is probable that his words or actions were also impelled by past experiences on his part and not at all planned to be directed at you. Both of you may be the innocent receivers of false impressions from past backgrounds. This often is true.

When you resent an individual, you are really letting your impression of that person operate your mind and emotions. You have for the moment signed away your freedom. You are now in bondage to unpleasant feelings. The image of the person in your mind is twisting you around its mental fingers, so that you cannot get it out of your mind. You are no longer a free agent. You are no longer standing on your own spiritual feet and affirming your control of life. The person or situation you resent runs you. I have known men to be run by their offices because they leave each night with a resentment of their work. Their offices dominate their emotions and keep them in a negative state. Other people are run by relatives they resent.

The Bible clearly states that God made man in His own image and after His own likeness and gave to man dominion of his world. As you evolve spiritually, you arrive at the conclusion that you cannot afford to let anyone confuse you. You cannot afford to have resentment, anger or fear as destructive elements in your consciousness. People who never would commit suicide fail to realize that they may be doing the same thing mentally and emotionally over a long period of time by their unconsciously vicious emotional patterns. You can destroy yourself through hate, resentment and suppressed anger. It may take fifty years to do this, but the law of mind has to produce your subconscious patterns in form. During those years your health and personal relationships will suffer.

The basic pattern of spiritual normalcy is to get along with everyone, to be happy in your work and to have a fundamental acceptance of the world as a good place in which to live effectively. It is divinely normal to have love and self-expression. Devote your awareness to these and your mind and emotions will operate more normally. Relate them often to negative situations and you will find a warping of your viewpoint taking place. Accentuation of negatives makes all positives secondary and that leads to general defeat. The universe is a positive system and only those who are clear most of the time on right attitudes can get from life all that it has to offer. The individual in whom positives are secondary is the one who psychologists label neurotic. A neurotic is anyone who allows the emotional structure of his nature to be released through negative outlets.

God made you a free man. Realize that you do not have to resent anyone and you can stop doing it. Appreciate yourself as a creative potential of mind and emotion. Without increasing the human ego, take your stand as a spiritually-dominated person who knows where you are going and will not let petty diversions of negative reactions becloud your pathway. As resentment is your reaction to someone, not the person himself, you can heal yourself of your own wrong reaction. Understanding why people behave as they do is essential if you are to live with a minimum of tension. The one causing you a disturbance cannot help doing it. Knowing this, you can cease your resentment, for you are only handling an emotional problem in yourself, you are not arguing with the person.

No person is under a compulsion to do you harm. Deep within everyone is a desire to be understood, appreciated and to give to others the best they can. All that the infinite Spirit asks of you is that you grow in consciousness and in usefulness as a human being. It does not demand that you put up with nonsense and give it a false label of humility. It asks you to rise in the dignity of your spiritual nature and live with authority over your experience. You then see the stupidity of resentment, for it allows the image of another person to govern your emotions. To handle resentment say to yourself:

I am one with all the Life, Love and Truth there is, for I am one with God. I am one with every person for in each is the image and likeness of perfect Life. I take full spiritual control of my mind and emotions, and I refuse to be disturbed by person or situation. No resentment can find acceptance in my consciousness. I have spiritual understanding of all whom I know. I behold in them the Love of God which blesses and benefits me. The actions and words of another person have no power nor authority within me. I am at peace with myself and with others. I am the only thinker in my world, and I guard my emotions night and day to maintain my freedom from others. The only relationship I can have with any person is one of love, understanding and peace. I am a free and uncluttered expression of God.

No resentment is worth the negative emotions nor the psychological twisting of your viewpoint which it will cause. There is always so much constructive living to do that the bypaths and detours of viciousness are stupid. The main road for the well-balanced man is straight ahead. It includes all who go the way with him, but if one or more cause reactions that becloud the vision, then the negatives must be met, so that the roadway is always clear. The wisdom in Jesus said to love our enemies, to do good to those who persecute and to keep going in the right direction. Let no man interfere with the spiritual necessity of your on-going.

A help in doing this is realizing that all life responds to recognition. The recognition of God as the center of your thinking and feeling causes extra power to act in you. The sages noticed that when they affirmed life, there was a response of increased life. Holding a resentment is a contracting experience. In the midst of it begin to affirm the action of love and understanding, and these will cause a response. What you recognize happens in your experience. The recognition of good in the midst of evil causes good to predominate over evil. Love will always conquer resentment, provided you determinedly recognize love in the persons you resent. They may never know that you are doing this, but it will clear you of the vicious feeling, and that is all that needs to be done. What happens to the other person is none of your business. Your business is to make certain which moods, feelings and impulses are dominating your consciousness. The thoughts and feel-ings of the other person have no power in you, but your own thinking and feeling does.

Jesus was never insulted by anyone, because he re-fused to receive their actions and words as insults. He had so cleared his consciousness that no man could cause him to indulge in resentment. His whole atten-tion was on the Spirit which acted through him and on ways in which to let this Spirit act. People did insult him, a man betrayed him. Yet, you find no condemnation in his words or actions. He knew that each person had to be what the sum-total of his consciousness contained. He also knew that until the other person really wanted to improve his consciousness there was little he could do. He never tried to change people through any outer means. If the ideas he spoke and practiced were not sufficient to inspire them to a higher way, then he knew there was nothing to do but wait until they were ready to change.

You cannot reform anyone you know. Reformation is a waste of time, energy and speech. The more you know a living presence of God in every man, the more you leave each person to find his own revelation. The older churches have been pressurizing people into states of grace for ages. It has never worked and it never will. You rise higher in life through your own choice. Preaching even this teaching to others is useless unless they ask for it with sincerity and simplicity. Most of the people you know want to hold on to their resentments in order to justify their own egos. Let them do this until they see the fallacy of it. Someday, somewhere, they will awaken to the fact that their job is to live in peace with themselves, and that others cannot destroy this inner peace without their inviting them to do so.

The more your consciousness expands through di-

rectly motivated thinking, the easier you will live with
more people in your world. They may never change
their viewpoints, and it is no concern of yours if they
don't, but you can always improve yours. The expression of Love is needed and you can express it. Not a
love which demands that the other person fit all your
requirements, but a love which leaves the other free to
evolve on his own pathways in his own time. We usually want the other person to improve at a greater
speed than his consciousness is able to do. Give every
man time to grow. You want others to let you make
your own decisions, so do the same for the friends
and loved ones in your life. Let God in them be their
impulsion and each will grow the faster as your re-
minders lessen.

The field of personal relationships is probably the
hardest to face with understanding. Most of us don't
even understand ourselves, yet we insist upon forcing
our viewpoints on others. The greatest spiritual understanding you can achieve is that of knowing that you
can control no man, but you must explore the depths
and inner meanings of yourself. This is the practice of
the old adage to live and let live. Every man has a god-
given right to think as he chooses. You may not agree
with his thinking, but you must allow him the right
to think that way.

Jesus said that he judged no man. He never judged
those who were unkind to him. He knew that his con-

sciousness was too busy doing the work he had been given to do to let such negatives handle him. Much resentment is followed by false judgement and human mind analysis. The hurt is followed by self-justification and the mind starts a process of witch-hunting to prove the hurt to be purposely inflicted. The other person is then examined and his faults magnified and his possible virtues annulled. This false judgement under resentment is a series of lies. Their power to enthrall is tremendous and the results of such wrong thinking is disastrous. If resentment enters your mind, think twice before you let it lodge there.

People are wonderful. Despite all their faults, they are the color and joy of living. We don't appreciate enough the warmth of knowing, working and living with people. The Divine Wisdom created them that they should have mutual understanding, mutual affection and mutual goals. That is why the religions of the world have taught the brotherhood of man. The reasons for our bickerings are so minor and the reasons for our mutual cooperation are so great. The dream of peace on earth and goodwill toward men is the God-potential in each man. One day this shall be, for we shall see the stupidity of our self-erected barriers of resentment, non-trust and ill-will.

There is glory in living which so many miss. There is the joy of good fellowship. People are God's grandest creations. They are your easiest means for giving and receiving love. Anything that lessens this ability should be erased. The purpose of evolution is growth, not only through lessons to be learned, but through triumphs to be achieved and joys to be experienced. Science has been gradually destroying the limitations which have prevented us from living fully. With all of Science's advances we cannot remain the small-minded people, we must move with Science to the larger plan of life.

In you is the love of God and the greatness of Being. Your ways of thinking determine how much of life can be yours. Letting go of the little, we can assume the great. Letting go of resentment, we can be the greater man that God planned. There is no power arrayed against us. God is the only real power and the only real presence, and all of God acts in our minds. In the long run, we can afford not to resent for the goal ahead is more important than the impediments along the way. Our hurts are excess baggage which we carry. They need to be thrown away that we may travel far while traveling light.

5

The Divine Intangible

ALL THAT MAKES life worthwhile is intangible. Life,
love, mind, beauty, joy and even God are intangibles.
They are forever allusive to the five sense mind.
Though we experience phases of each, we sense that
more and greater experiences are possible. No one has
ever loved or been loved too much. No mind has ever
known all that it could know. The grandest theological
definitions of God never are complete. There is always
more to be known, felt and experienced. The Divine in
us always is giving us a thirst and a hunger for greater
truth.

God as the creative Mind is a cosmic necessity. Life
is far too well organized to have created itself. With
all man's cleverness he cannot create half as well as the
Infinite Planner does. No man has ever seen God. He
has seen people who acted the way he thought God
must act, and these men he has named saviours, saints
and messiahs. Their minds, hearts and accomplish-

ments were symbols of man's own inner possibilities.

Not believing in a man-God is not as simple as it seems. It is easy to throw the concept of an elderly gentleman on a throne in heaven out the window, but to find a replacement that satisfies your soul is another project. No man can long be an atheist for his world about him bespeaks a deity. God as a cosmic intangible lacks appeal for many people. They need their holy symbols of a greater man to remind them of the fullness that life can be. Yet, the growth of true spiritual understanding is dependent upon moving in consciousness from a tangible and therefore limited God to an intangible, unlimited Mind. It is the most important progressive action you ever will make.

The older religions had to teach a material concept of God, as the people in those days could not comprehend a Power that acted without personality. Their religion had to supply them with a god which could be understood with their five sense thinking. Later religions kept this God made in the image and after the likeness of man, but for their followers who were emancipating themselves from limited beliefs, they added the philosophical intangible concept. This second theological premise was accepted by the enlightened and the spiritually daring, because they perceived a universal creative spiritual process in everything. Most religions of recent centuries have included both systems of thought. Many of the readers of this book will realize that through the years they have accepted both ideas at the same time and not realized it.

In the last three hundred years and particularly in the last hundred years, there have appeared several organized churches whose sole purpose is to teach the God of intangibles and to lay aside forever any and all speculations of God as a man. The Quakers, Unitarians, Universalists and the Metaphysical bodies have led the way in presenting this larger viewpoint. It has been a long hard road. Most people still want their traditional spiritual props. They never think to modernize their religious life the way they do their homes. They surround themselves with every up to date comfort, but their spiritual understanding is usually three hundred years behind the times.

Modern religion has but one primary idea to present. It teaches that God is an infinite spiritual Intelligence or Mind in action through all creation, and particularly in action in man. The creative power around man is impersonal law, but in man it acts in a personal way. God personalizes and individualizes Itself in man. This larger viewpoint will not appeal to those who need a god to justify their illnesses, bankruptcies and trials. It most certainly will not appeal to those who want an after death heaven and hell. Many people cannot accept the law of cause and effect as a spiritual one, because it makes them do too much inner probing to find the reasons for their failures.

Life is the capacity to create what you want and to strive toward what you want to be. Spirit is the inner capacity to create and Mind provides the pattern of what you want to be. Heaven and hell are symbols of the good and bad effects of your own thinking. As the creative power in you does not know either age nor circumstance, you always can create what you want and become the individual you would like to be. There is no aspect of God which can oppose Its creation, so always you are free to do and become what you choose. God in you, as your consciousness, awaits your recognition to move into full creative action through you. You can do this by saying to yourself:

I am forever a part of the living Spirit. The creative power of God indwells me and acts through me. This word which I now declare is the law of perfect action. The full action of Infinite Mind now moves through my consciousness and accomplishes the desires of my heart. In me God is my health, peace, love and self-expression. In my world God is order, harmony and ever-expanding good. I recognize myself as the inlet and outlet of God, the one eternal Mind.

This larger understanding is as old as the first liberal philosopher and most philosophers taught some ideas similar to this. In religion, it is new, fresh and radical. It is appealing to millions who are able to take the step from a tangible limited god to an intangible un-limited Spirit. Ideas are the symbols and straight think-ing is the ritual of the new thought of God and the larger thought of man. The more you divorce yourself from limiting the creative power, and the more you know yourself as that power in action, the greater your achievements spiritually, mentally, emotionally and materially.

The intangible Spirit and Mind of the eternal One are omnipresent. Where you are at every split second the perfect action is taking place. Being everywhere, it is in all. From the lowliest material object to the greatest intellect, there is but one grand ascending scale of mental action. Somewhere along this scale you will find yourself. As the scale is an ascending one, you are on a pathway of ever-expanding consciousness. You move from glory to glory. Your present affairs are alive with the Divine Intangible which is all intelli-gence, love and orderly action. Your body is radiant with its vitality, power and beauty. You walk the ways of this earth as the Intangible made Tangible.

This ascending program of living requires the con-stant acceptance and expectation of the next accom-plishment to be made. When the artist finishes his painting of a picture, his mind is already planning another one. Most authors when they hand their com-pleted manuscript to their publisher, start planning their next book. This is the way the intangible Spirit in you works. What is next on your list to do and to be? Use your present aliveness, your present ideas and feelings to create your present good, but know your next idea to fulfill. As your mind is a part of the one Mind, it works according to the same principle. The infinite creative Mind is forever making all things new. That is the principle upon which It works. It never tries to maintain things as they are. It has finished with these as soon as they have been completed. God is always working on the next project. You have to do the same if you are to play your full role in life.

The divine Mind will always be conceiving new ideas. These are yours for the taking. They do not enter the negative mind. Fear, resentment and other vicious attitudes hold fast the door against the inflow of spiritual impulses. Faith, vision and right thinking unlock the door of consciousness and release the flood of creative thought. Just as Mind will always be creating ideas of greater good, so will the material universe around you be ready and able to translate these ideas into actual forms and situations. Your mind is the link between heaven and earth. Your consciousness can take in new ideas, accept them, and give them to the subconscious to become form in matter. Thus, you are the vehicle through which the Intangible becomes tangible.

Let new ideas work in your mind and new things and situations take place in your world. If you live with spiritual intent your world is always changing for the better, because you are always using better ideas in your consciousness. The creative Mind is never static, never depleted and never confused. Think the same way and you will never have fears again. Consciousness needs to be shaken up, cleaned out and put in order as much as your house or office needs to have an occasional thorough cleaning. With an orderly fresh viewpoint, the larger ideas appear and you grasp them with joy and plan their extension into form with ease.

The infinite Mind which will always know more than you know consistently offers you the means for knowing more than you know this moment. This is the way of growth. The possibility of improvement is in everything you do. You may be healthy, but you can be even healthier. You may have a good income, but you can prosper more. You may have enough friends and loved ones, but more nice people can be in your social life. The plus element is unlimited when you link your thinking with the mind of God and work on the side of the new, and fret not if the old dies out of your life. This is the life more abundant promised you from of old. Be one of those who grasp it, rejoice in it and let it happen.

The present world offers you a super-abundance. There are more good things available to more people in these present times than ever before in the history of the world. Never before in any civilization has there been such invention, production and distribution of things with as many people financially able to buy them and appreciate them. Mankind has evolved and earned this freedom in things. Yet, you may be one of those who lives with less ease than you did twenty years ago. If this is true, then you are not progressing spiritually. Somewhere in your consciousness a block has been established. Some warping of either your thinking or your feeling has caused you to step aside from the creative process of living. You rest in your limitation, while the great cosmic creative process goes on and others flow with it and benefit from their co-operation with it.

Throw yourself into the midstream of creative living. Be not content with the half when the whole of life is yours. God's ideas come to you as much as they do to any man. God has no special people, and plays no favorites. The sun shines on the limited and the free; the rich and the poor; the happy and the tragic. The intangible perfect action of Truth gives equally to all whom It has created as operative processes of Itself. Stop recognizing yourself as limited, and look out and behold what you can be. You are the only determining factor in your life. I cannot withhold your good, nor can anyone. If your consciousness is vitally aware of God and His great ideas, there is neither person, situation nor circumstance that can stop you from having a creative experience.

Ideas are your most precious commodity. They determine the length and breadth of your consciousness. These intangibles impoverish you or prosper you. The metaphysician seeks for ideas in everything and every situation. He knows that the infinite Mind is in all and through all revealing right action. As simple an object as a coffee pot is an idea in form. Hundreds of ideas went into the designing, planning and production of it. Think of the mind action that went into its construction. Think of your own mind action as you selected it, paid for it and had it delivered to your home. Your mind is in action with this same idea every time you use the coffee pot. As you search for ideas in things, you discover your world to be a flexible one. Back of the solidarity of forms is the flexible flow of the Spirit with its tremendous field of ideas awaiting your recognition.

Isaiah wrote that the trees could clap their hands. He visioned the movement of their branches in a severe storm like people applauding a performance. He saw the trees giving praise to that Mind which made them. "For ye shall go out with joy, and be led forth with peace; the mountains and the hills shall break forth before you with singing, and all the trees of the field shall clap their hands." (Isaiah 55:12) He knew that our five senses report only a part of the true experience of life. We see, hear, taste, touch and smell only a portion of all that life offers to us. People sit for hours before a great painting to absorb the infinite variety of ideas the masterpiece offers. Music lovers can hear a great opera many times each season and never fail to get new ideas from its music. The people with whom you live, work and associate socially have depths of vital interest that you never completely can probe. To each of us the world offers all that it is. Too often we are but beggars at the gate of heaven, when the Mind of God gives us all that we can assimilate. You live, move and have your being in the inexhaustible Mind of creation.

"For unto everyone that hath shall be given, and he shall have abundance; but from him that hath not shall be taken away even that which he hath." (Matthew 25:29) The creative consciousness constantly receives fresh ideas. The stilted mind becomes increasingly less creative as its monotonies cripple it. The brilliant become more brilliant. The stupid become more stupid. Both types of consciousness operate in the same universal Mind. One sees life as the interplay of thought and feeling. The other sees only the material world of forms and is deluded by them. Investigate your thinking for the past few days and see whether life is making you richer in ideas or poorer in perspectives.

Everything is mental as well as physical. You are consciousness using a body. The objective world is not only form but idea. To see only the form and fail to know the idea is like a person looking at a sheet of music, but never hearing it played. The sages have looked at the earth and yet seen heaven shining through. They never have permitted themselves to be ensnared in things and gains. They enjoyed things and accepted gains but kept their vision on the grand interplay of consciousness. Moses looked at a few thousand slaves in Egypt and at the same time beheld a free nation. Jesus looked at a cross but kept his thinking on eternal life. He told his followers that they had eyes but saw not and ears that heard not. He knew that there was more to life than outer accomplishments and more to death than a corpse. His expanding consciousness held true to divine ideas, and his thinking still is lifting the world.

The omnipresence of perfect Mind is the reality of being. Its unceasing action as ideas in man's consciousness is his sure salvation. The more you affirm the presence and the power of Mind in your life, the greater your progress in living life scientifically. Say to yourself:

There is only one Mind, God, and my world is saturated with divine ideas that lead me every step of my way. No more indecision, mistakes nor wrong judgements. My consciousness is a center of perfect Intelligence in that Mind which is God. The action of God's Ideas in my thinking is now complete. I know what I need to know at the instant I need to know it. My consciousness is ever expanding in its scope and interest. I let divine Ideas govern my thinking and divine Love govern my feelings. I am the unlimited outlet of an unlimited Mind.

The above is practicing scientific prayer. Such right thinking sets up new causation in your mind. It creates new points of beginnings, new points of departures into larger vistas of mind action which, in turn, create larger experiences in the world of form. If you treat your thinking by making statements like those above several times each day you will find old conditions passing away and new situations being born. Scientific prayer is spiritual treatment. As a surgeon removes a false growth from the body, so does treatment remove old negatives from consciousness. Its daily practice is spiritual life insurance.

At the beginning of this chapter, I mentioned the new and better understanding of God which is changing the viewpoints of millions. With this new concept of the infinite creative Intangible, there appeared a new form of prayer. Beseeching a creative Mind and Spirit was discovered a useless device and the new form of prayer, based on scientific mental statements, was developed. In scientific prayer you manipulate states of consciousness in yourself infusing into them spiritual ideas which transform them into creative operating

centers. You deny all negatives by saying they ca[...]
be. You then affirm the spiritual positive you want to
experience.

The divine Intangible uses your mind as a center for
Its operation. To your consciousness It gives the fullness of Itself. You need never plead again for your
good to happen. Pleading to a God is a waste of
energy, and it usually only increases the problem you
want dissolved. The ideas which will solve your problem are already in your mind, for the divine Mind has
placed them there. Your denial of the problem and
your affirmation of having the right idea to solve it,
causes that divine Idea to reveal Itself in your thinking.
Being a divine Idea, It is self-empowered to direct your
subconscious to produce for you the dissolution of an
evil and the creation of a good.

The Intangible becomes tangible by means of you.
You are the means by which the Infinite releases Its
ideas into form. Every time you think creatively you
are honoring your God. Every time you behold goodness in others and in yourself you are praising your
Creator. The destruction of negatives and the bringing
forth of positives is the true spiritual way of life. This
is what every world Teacher has taught. He has revealed the Truth that consciousness is all there really
is, and that salvation is nothing more or less than right
use of mind. This will read like heresy to many, but
it is the truth.

The man God made indwells you and operates as you. You are in a stream of life which is divinely originated, divinely promoted and divinely directed. The universal Mind seeks your evolution to higher plateaus of living. Emerge from the crystalization of your present set opinions into the larger mind and the greater life. Having free will you can delay your good as long as you wish, but eventually the larger ideas will appeal to you, and you will move forward.

If you accept current opinions, do only those things which society says are correct and remain in the conventional grooves, you never can know the omnipresence of the glory of Mind and Its ideas. To believe in the Mind of God and to accept yourself as Its vehicle takes courage. It makes you an explorer of consciousness. It requires mental and emotional discipline that is far from easy. It demands a mental diet of right ideas, so that your consciousness is nourished with the right type of substance to create for you the kind of world you want to live in.

The possibilities of what you can demonstrate through this science are unlimited. "Eye hath not seen, nor ear heard, neither have entered into the heart of man, the things which God hath prepared for them that love him." (I Corinthians 2:9) The unlimited ideas of the infinite Mind are yours to draw upon. Your understanding of life as a spiritual experience is your love for God. This opens to you the floodgates of heavenly ideas. This erases all fear of the future, for you can create the future you want. It releases you from all dependence on others, for in your spiritual independence you create what you need when you need it. Out of the Intangible with all Its blessings there comes to you, as Its beloved intention, the riches of the kingdom of heaven, the kingdom of unconditioned, perfect God Ideas.

6

The Intangible and Business

YOU START IN business the moment you are born. Life doesn't wait until you are an adult to put you in business. Business is activity specialized for the production of a creative good. The distinction between life and death is activity. Being alive means you are in business. This does not describe business in the usual economic terms, yet actual profit making business is also activity specialized for the production of a good. The action of Life is the result of the ceaseless movement of the infinite Mind within Itself creating ideas of Itself which It releases through aspects of Itself and you are one of the aspects of God.

Business is the activity necessary for an idea to become form and that form to be used. This describes all types of business but it also describes the workings of your mind. Your mental processes are the means by which ideas become form. Your conscious area of mind selects ideas, gives them to the subconscious and the subconscious proceeds to produce them in form. This creative process is the premise upon which all spiritual demonstration takes place. Your consciousness is your business. The way you use your consciousness determines whether your life is evidencing good business or bad.

Many people worry about their income-producing business. They watch over it with great care but they fail to watch their trends of thinking with similar care. They blame poor business on world conditions, instead of changing their thought so that better business could be created. Worry over business is one of the most respectable forms of negation there is today. The non-worried business man is a rarity. If you take fear out of your mind your profits will increase. Fear subtly destroys the very creative ideas that you need in order to prosper. Metaphysically your business is the projection of your thinking, and it will prosper only when your mind is spiritually positive.

Every person is in business. The housewife and mother is in business. The child is in business. You may never work an hour of your life and have great income, but you are still in business. You have to run a home, drive a car and socialize with others. Some believe that at the age of sixty-five they retire from business. They only retire from an income-producing activity. They then have more time to be busier about other things. The chronic worrier has more time to do the business of worrying and an exhaustive business that is. The creative person takes his extra freedom to create in other ways. His positive consciousness must continue producing positive results in life.

Assuming that you work in an office, a factory or shop only describes the outer economic structure which has been established because of an idea. A business is an idea. Large or small it is an idea in action. Being an idea, it is dependent on consciousness far more than it is dependent upon either inflation or depression. Many readers won't readily believe this but it is true. An idea is dependent only on the action of the creative Mind for its operation, maintenance, development and future. The business man able to perceive the idea in his business always can keep a flow of creative activity prospering that business. Automatically, the larger Mind reveals right ideas at the right time to him. If you know you are working with an idea, then you do not over-emphasize the facts of income and disbursements. You do not make these the sole end of your thinking.

A ledger never defines your business. It shows what you do with it. It may show the cleverness of your human mind, but the true measurement of any business is in its ability to produce something of value to your fellowman. If it is not doing this, then all the tricks of material thinking won't save it from destruction. Every great business has been built on an idea, plus faith in that idea. Your job seemingly may be a minor one in a great corporation, but the above holds true. Your value to your company is in direct ratio to your being sold on the idea of the company and having faith in that idea. The housewife must believe in her home as an idea and think of it in creative terms to have a warm, loving atmosphere in it. The child must have faith in his parents in order to express activity in creative ways that will build a healthy future.

Every time you forget the central idea in what you are doing and work only with the outer details, pressures and problems, you exhaust yourself. Material thinking not backed up by a spiritual vision is the most depleting process any man ever will know. It wears out the body, it fills the mind with fears and it takes all pleasure out of living. "Where there is no vision the people perish: but he that keepeth the law, happy is he." (Proverbs 29:18) The law of infinite Mind is a law of ideas moving ceaselessly from thought to form. This is the law of all good business. This is the basic law of prosperity, health and creative self-expression. I have seen businesses and business men fail merely from losing the perspective of the central idea and concentrating all their attention on problems. The law of mind action delivers to you what you consistently think. No business can prosper with unnappy, worried and confused employees. No man can prosper in his work if his consciousness is beset with negatives.

Jesus said that there was a way of working that was easy and a labor that was light. I am certain that the way he spoke about was one of holding fast to the main idea of business and letting that idea unfold its own major and minor aspects. All ideas come to you from the universal Mind completely equipped to demonstrate themselves. They unfold in your quiet thinking and make clear the ways and means of fulfilling themselves. At least once each day rest a moment from your human mind struggle to achieve and say to yourself something like this:

My business is God's business and it is owned, operated and expanded by Divine Ideas. The exactly right idea which I need for this day now unfolds in my consciousness. Coming from the Divine Intelligence it has within it every lesser idea I need to know. I now let this right idea govern my thinking. I am open and receptive to new angles, new perspectives and new plans. God as Mind knows what I need to know and I am one with all Mind, so I now know all that I need to know.

People who work all their lives without a spiritual understanding of business are like Adam. They eat of the tree of good and evil ideas and like him they work by the sweat of their brows. They work only for money or prestige or power. Little that they accomplish is creative, for the flow of new ideas is not in them. Their sole aim is to work as few hours as possible to get the most money possible. They have no ideals in regard to their work, and they receive no pleasure from their work. Every industry has such workers on their pay rolls.

Ideals and ideas are the mental food of the spiritually conscious person. They are as necessary to the mind as food and clothing is to the body. An ideal is not a fantasy. Ideals impel you to action, while a fantasy charms the mind and does nothing more. Many people who think they have a great ideal really have a pleasant fantasy because it never causes them to do any actual creative work. An ideal impels you to do something that not only enriches you but adds some good to other people. A fantasy is always a self-centered idea.

The spiritually wise have suggested that money was not a sufficient reason for working. If your whole attention is on getting money from your work, you are out of balance. A backward step in the economy of the present age was taken when most employees exaggerated the two items of time and money. People want jobs with easy hours and quick money. We need to reinstitute the value of ideals and ideas in our business structure to keep it a healthy one.

Money is not a cure-all. It is a valuable means of living with ease and having what you want. It is a spiritual thing and every person should prosper. It is a circulation of the good. Satisfaction in your work will produce more money more easily and at the same time maintain you in psychological health. It is a tragedy to note the people who dislike their jobs. Yet, suggest that they change to some work that they would like and they start their usual list of alibis. Usually, it is the short hours, good pay and a retirement plan which keeps them in their jobs. Spiritually, none of these three are good reasons at all. It means that they may prosper materially and at the same time impoverish themselves spiritually.

What do you take to your business of living each morning? You take your consciousness. An important new development in many large corporations is the establishing of psychological counsellors and in some cases psychologically trained clergymen. They are doing this because they realize that workers who are not happy within themselves cannot do an effective day's work. By making available to them these services the corporations are doing a healthy thing. Check your psychological approach to your work and see if it is a constructive one. If it isn't, then you had better do something radical about it. Either re-establish the ideal or think of changing your work to one which will include an ideal. You cannot afford to hate your work for very long.

Your consciousness is the tool you take to your job. It determines the day you will have and the accomplishments you will make. It will affect those who work with you. No matter how carefully you try not to show your mood, it becomes obvious to others. Each day is an opportunity to be creative, dynamic and helpful. The infinite Mind gives us each twenty-four hours to use as a laboratory in which to experiment with ideas, ideals and moods. The day is too valuable to be wasted on unpleasantness. It is a day you will never see again. During the day your moods and experiences register in your subconscious mind and add to the sum total of memory. In turn this added memory affects the tones of your consciousness the next day. It is an endless series. But, the negative angles of your subconscious moods can be changed and then your surface moods improve.

Take one spiritual idea each morning and think it through, mull it over as you go to your work. It will do far more for your consciousness than vitamins will do for your body. It is a valuable capsule which will enrich your consciousness and make easier your job. This is good therapy. It quickens ideas. It makes you rejoice as you see ideas moving to become form. It lessens the tensions and increases your faith. As an example try the following the first thing in the morning for a week:

Life is activity; it is business. God is life and I am the action of the life of God. I am a center of intelligence in the mind of God. Today, I work with ease. I let Divine Ideas function in my thinking. I let Divine Love govern my emotions. I shall accomplish through the power of God that indwells me. I like my work, my co-workers and my responsibilities. Through these I give value to life and in turn I am of value to God.

"Every man also to whom God hath given riches and wealth, and hath given him power to eat thereof, and to take his portion, and to rejoice in his labor; this is the gift of God." (Ecclesiastes 5:19) With an uplifted consciousness you still put in the number of hours needed, you still earn the much needed money, but you have a good reason for doing it, and you have a greater ease in the doing of it. Use the time-money structure through which you function, but never again make it the end as well as the means. This takes you from the level of labor to the level of creative work. You cease being the Adam man and start being the creative individual that Life planned you to be.

People have come to me for counsel and have told me that they hated their jobs, hated their associates and hated the companies for whom they worked. Unfortunately, there are thousands of people in such states of mind, and only a few of them make any effort to change their thinking. My discussion with these people leads to one basic question. Why do they hate anything? Hate is an abnormal diversion of the capacity to love. Listening to their life histories I usually find that they always have resented any work they ever have done. This means that unconsciously, for a variety of reasons peculiar to each person, there has been established in his or her subconscious mind a resentment to the fact that he has to work. There is a feeling that the world owes that person a living. Spiritual understanding usually clears up this false concept. You cannot escape the business of living, no matter how hard you try. Hating what you do only ties you more completely to it. It means that you are allowing a strong negative dislike to rule your thinking for a minimum of eight hours a day. It is probably more like sixteen hours a day, because you carry your dislike into your free time and it still colors your consciousness.

An ideal in some form is in the place where you work, and you can find it, if you really want to find it. If hate and resentment have dominated your thinking for a long time, you will not even try to find a good in that which you label as evil. Yet, the good is there. God is omnipresent His whole creation through, and this includes the place where you work and the people with whom you work. You spend one third of your life working and if that third is unhappy then the other two thirds are colored by that unhappiness. To be wholesome in its better spiritual sense you need to be at peace in every major area of life. It is impossible to be happy in one or two areas of life and bitterly unhappy in another. They coalesce into one consciousness and all are affected. Worried business men do not have happy home lives. Nor can men unhappy at home be happy at the office. All moods flow through all areas of action.

Where you work, you are needed, particularly if you have a spiritual understanding of business. You can be the leaven unto the whole loaf. You need never mention your spiritual beliefs and your practice of them but your moods will affect the other workers. What you are on the inside will evidence itself on the outside. If you are creative, ambitious and wise, it will be obvious. The others may be working under what today is called the normal pressures of business. Strange that we have come to a place where extreme pressures are considered normal. Yet, you will be noticed for the way you accomplish without strain. Knowing that God in you is the ability to do what needs to be done without pressure, you radiate a quiet, effective confidence.

There is an interesting fact about your subconscious mind that is valuable to know. It exists in a universal Subconscious in which the sum total of the world

thinking since man began is functioning. At the subconscious level you are one with all knowledge past
and present. Plus this group knowledge there also is in
the universal subconscious an immense Intelligence.
In other words there not only is a great wisdom, there
is also the intelligence to take this wisdom and do
something with it. Dr. Carl Jung, the noted psycho-
analyst writes: "I have to admit the fact that the unconscious mind is capable at times of assuming an
intelligence and purposiveness which are superior to
actual conscious thought." * Thus, any idea you subconsciously accept operates in a field of tremendous
intelligence and wisdom which can produce for you
results beyond what your conscious mind ever could
plan.

This will explain the statement of Jesus—"All power
is given unto me in heaven and in earth." (Matthew
28:18) He intuitively sensed that his ideas and words
were produced into form by a power larger than himself. His ideas went into the subconscious where a
greater Intelligence knew what to do to accomplish
their fulfillment. This plus element of the subconscious
is of great importance to a business person. It means
that as they work a larger Intelligence works through
them and that they can quicken this larger Mind by
recognizing that it is working. Just to say to yourself:

* *Psychology and Religion,* page 45.

In me is the Universal Mind which knows far more than I do. I let this great subconscious knowing and acting power do for me this day what I need to do this day. All the wisdom, wit and intelligence of God now is working through me to accomplish what I plan to do.

Assume an idea about your business of living. Assume an ideal about each major area of your life. One for your work, another for your home, another for your family, etc. Think of these ideals with conscientious sincerity. This establishes them in your subconscious where the Mind of God takes them over and in Its own ways makes them factual in your experience. You will discover that your present pressures will diminish. You will have greater wisdom and a larger freedom. You will soon feel that you are in your right place, doing your right work. Eventually, you will arrive at the high spiritual peak where you can say "I do not work for money. I work for the glory of God and the money happens as a result." This is the great goal of business. This means you have a creative consciousness; you are respected by others and you are praised for your accomplishments.

Right attitudes can make a business. Wrong attitudes can destroy a business. The future can never be planned with certainty. The best laid plans of individuals and corporations go astray. Assume that the

Divine Mind which has brought you this far will take you the rest of the way. With this right attitude the future will unfold with a minimum of difficulties. The infinite Mind always is conceiving new ideas for you to explore and experience. Refuse to believe that your job is static or has no future. If you will let in the Divine Ideas that impinge on your consciousness, you will move steadily forward. They will either change your present work for the better, or they will reveal to you another work where your expansion of creativeness can take place. God never binds any man to an intolerable situation.

The universe is activity whether the physicist resolves it into forms of energy mathematically operating, or the metaphysician sees it as Mind becoming form, or the theologian sees it as heaven becoming earth. It is all one thing. Where you work, you are specializing this activity in a unique way for certain results. You are one with the eternal action of the Mind and Heart of God. You have a right to make a profit out of your work. You have a right to be happy while you are working. You have a right to leave your day's work and have a sense of accomplishment. All this is dependent on your own thinking about yourself and your work. Others may advise, but you, as the only thinker in your mind, determine your relationship with business.

The years ahead can be bright with promise or foredoomed to bitterness. The responsibility is not on the shoulders of God, nor on the insistence of your rights. In you is the capacity to live with ease, accomplish mightily and create wonderfully. Use it you may and not use it you can. God's perfect action of Mind indwells you. It offers Itself to you and bids you partake of the satisfactions of work. You will never be completely happy until you work with joy. You may alibi until time ends but the truth prevails that some work with the joy of accomplishment because they have ideals with which to be stimulated. In the home, the office, the community, wherever you work, there is an Ideal to be found and a Purpose to be discovered. Finding these and applying them to your work bring the crown of glory, a crown that can never be measured in money. You may die rich or poor but if the crown is yours you die at peace in the world to which you have given much.

7

Why Spiritual Thinking Heals

A COMMON SENSE disciplining of your thought and feeling will heal you, provided you realize that both thought and feeling are the creative powers of the Spirit within you. Without the spiritual premise that you are a phase and function of the infinite Intelligence, you cannot heal yourself or others. It is essential to know that God heals, but not through a miracle. You exist in a world of mind action that operates through a law of cause and effect. Disease is the result of a cause unconsciously established in the subconscious mind of the person ill. It is no longer a mystery. Illness is a normal effect from an abnormal cause.

Human thought and feeling will not heal. The field of psychology uses the human mind to change the human mind, and achieves very few physical results from its methods. It will give self-understanding, self-acceptance and remove a great deal of guilt, but its work in physical healing is minor. The modern meta-physical movements have healed millions of people through their instruction that God is the mind and emotion of each person and that this mind and emotion can be spiritually used to conquer disease. By recognizing yourself, including your body, as an action of the Divine Mind, you are able to heal.

The Infinite is completely individualized in every person. What God does on the grand scale of the cosmos, It does in the more limited area of your consciousness. The cosmic order is the result of an originating Mind acting through law to produce and maintain form. In you, this spiritual process acts to maintain you in health. Unimpeded by human mind obstructions this normal and natural activity would maintain you always as a healthy expression of Itself. Health is divinely normal and sickness is humanly abnormal.

In most of the ancient religions healing was practiced as a divine art. Their priests were the only medical practitioners of their day. Sick people went to their temples or churches and the priests acted as their doctors as well as their spiritual guides. In the early period of Hebrew history the priesthood served both purposes. Many of the health laws to be found in the book of Leviticus in the Old Testament prove this to be so. However, in Jesus' time healing was not practiced by the Jewish Church and its priesthood. Therefore, the importance of Jesus' technique of spiritual healing should have been given the greatest emphasis. A large section of the writings about Jesus describe not only the healings he accomplished but also the technique he imparted to others.

Few people realize that Christianity should have been founded as a system of spiritual mind healing, instead of merely a system of salvation. If you haven't read the four biographies of Jesus in the New Testament in a long time, do so. They reveal the importance that healing had in the thinking of Jesus. Repeatedly, he told his disciples to go forth and heal the sick as well as preach the good tidings of man's spiritual heritage. Following the death of Jesus his disciples continued to heal and during all the first four hundred years of Christianity the practice of spiritual mind healing was a prominent part of the teaching. Around 400 A.D. the church dropped all healing and taught only its theological doctrines.

Sporadically through the centuries there have appeared slight revivals of the practice of healing, but they have never gained real prominence. Today, some of the orthodox churches show a slight interest in healing by spiritual therapy, but as far as I have been able to find these present day attempts offer no real importance nor value. Some churches have added psychiatrists to their staffs or set up psychological clinics. Patients who have been to several of these report that their main emphasis is on psycho-therapy with a slight indication that prayer will help the patient also. In other words, they are not trying to practice the healing methods of Jesus; they are attempting to combine psycho-therapy with theology, and that is a combination of oil and vinegar. It will never coalesce.

Spiritual healing based on Jesus' methods was given again to the world about 1860 through the study and practice of Phineas Parkhurst Quimby of Portland, Maine. The investigation of this gentle man revealed the true science behind healing. As a result of his work, spiritual healing is again available to all. The modern metaphysical churches have revived primitive christianity and their rapid expansion and growth gives evidence that the public is seeking and finding results in this new-old system, based on the teachings of the New Testament amplified with the understanding of Mind as cause and Form as effect. The world is again conscious of the fact that the healing power of the Spirit can be employed. Medicine and psychology can never be ignored, but the values of both can be increased by a correct knowledge of God and of Man.

Illness is the result of disorderly patterns in the subconscious. These patterns gradually develop from the emotional stress of life and can be psychologically diagnosed and spiritually cleared. Where there is order and balance at the subconscious level, health will be obvious in the body. In a previous chapter I have shown how the subconscious can always be changed by the conscious. You are equipped by the Infinite to express life fully. To do this you have to understand that your consciousness acts as a law; not under a law, but as a law. Cause becomes effect because a law operates. Your consciousness not only is the creative factor in your life, it is also the law which executes your moods, beliefs and convictions. It is your consciousness alone which makes you sick, and it is the establishing of order in your consciousness which makes you well. Your body is the first area of life to be affected by your thinking and feeling. It displays the effects of your consciousness obviously. You know how fear affects your appetite, etc.

The cells in your body do not make themselves sick. The body is not a causative process. Body is the screen upon which the pictures of your subconscious patterns appear. Your consciousness acting as a law determines your health or disease, and you have within you the power to direct your thinking and feeling to any end. It is the nature of Life to repair itself. Inherent in you is a restorative action seeking to maintain perfect, well balanced patterns in the subconscious. This is the indwelling Spirit. Your consciousness and body both have in them a healing intelligence which responds to your affirmative knowledge of God and of yourself as God's creation. The more you affirm that you are a spiritual expression of life, the less authority disease will have in your mind. Say to yourself:

am the Life and Mind of God in action. Through my consciousness the Infinite is living Itself as thought and feeling. I now affirm my spiritual nature as the beloved expression of all that God is. I am the health, life, vitality and perfect function of the Divine Mind. Every negative, confused and disease-causing pattern in my subconscious is now erased, nullified and destroyed by this treatment which is the word of God declared into the law of God. My health is definite, eternal and indestructible. I rejoice, give thanks and am glad.

Affirming perfect life enables it to operate the way it was intended to operate. That is why scientific prayer is affirmative. It lets God be God. It does not tell Life what to do; it lets Life under Its own intelligence do what needs to be done. Didn't you have somewhere in your family a relative who "took her to bed" whenever she felt the slightest indication of sickness? She rested for days and ate nothing but tea and toast. Soon she was as healthy as could be. In other words, she let Life be in her what Life was already equipped to be. The healing restorative action was given free reign, and she was without fear, as this was the method she had always used, and it had always worked. She took to her bed in faith and let God do the perfect work that Life accomplishes in its own normal ways.

Another important reason why scientific prayer heals

the sick is that it releases divine Intelligence in the subconscious which re-arranges the patterns, destroys the fears, eliminates human opinions, and gives new directions to consciousness. It causes that which already is, because it always has been, to be given freedom of action. The nature of God in the individual responds to the affirmation of Its presence. "Let the weak say, I am strong." (Joel 3:10) The natural order and activity of consciousness is creative. When this natural process is inhibited and mis-directed, illness results. Both sickness and health are mental states objectified in the body. Prayer deals with mental states and its power to heal is endless.

The Intelligence in you does not know degrees of sickness. It cannot differentiate between curability and incurability. As this divine Intelligence deals only with your consciousness, it does not know the physical symptoms nor the medical verdicts, nor your own negative speculations. God only knows Itself in you as perfect life. Therefore, your constant thinking in terms of an illness, your acceptance of the medical verdict and your further false speculations as to complications makes no impression on the Life that lives in you, but because these conditions are strongly accepted in consciousness, the Intelligence is being given wrong direction and the illness is not healed.

When you are sick watch your thinking and your speaking. There is no reason why the indwelling Spirit should alter the law of its own action to let you think and talk disease and at the same time make you well. You have to comply with the indwelling Spirit by working the way It works to get results. It responds to your attitudes. A constant thinking and speaking of symptoms keeps your consciousness maintaining present ones and creating new ones. The Law produces the material you give It. Think and talk what you want to experience. That is why scientific prayer heals. It redirects the mind of the patient from negatives to affirmatives. It replaces attention on the body with attention on God's Ideas. It diverts the consciousness long enough for the inherent Intelligence to act as a law of health.

Anything you do to spiritualize your thinking will cause a degree of healing. People have been healed by reading the Bible, attending a metaphysical lecture, and reading inspirational literature. Undoubtedly, this book will heal a number of people, as did my previous one. No one will ever know the healings that have taken place during concerts of great music, exhibitions of great paintings or the humor created by comedians. It is well known what a vacation away from your usual haunts will accomplish. All of these are devices to change the thinking of the person from a repetition of negatives to an anticipation of affirmatives.

Spiritual healing is being practiced by many of the fundamentalist churches with a good degree of success.

Several evangelists are appearing regularly on tele-
vision and their emotionally intense prayers for the
sick seem to produce tremendous results. Their whole
theology and preaching are exactly the opposite of the
teaching in this book, yet they get results. Watching
one of these men, and particularly listening to him,
you can see why the healing takes place. Through great
emotion and with deep spiritual faith, he arrives at the
conviction that the Spirit in the patient has healed the
patient, so the Law of Mind does heal the patient. His
belief demonstrates. It is obvious that the patient does
little to help him, as always the patient is astonished to
find himself better. The evangelist has intuitively and
unconsciously practiced spiritual mind healing. His
vocabulary and form of prayer are the exact opposite
of metaphysics. He beseeches Jesus to heal. He pleads
with God to come down from heaven and heal. But,
he gets results because he arrives at a subconscious
conviction of the perfection of his patient.

The professional practitioner of spiritual mind healing does the same thing, but more easily. He does not
need an intense emotional atmosphere in which to
work. Nor, does he beseech a distant deity to do the
work. He calmly knows and feels that the life in the
patient is God and that the divine Intelligence in the
patient's subconscious is free to act. The practitioner
uses a series of mental arguments known as denials
and affirmations. He uses these to convince himself

that God in the patient is health, and therefore disease does not exist any more. His conviction causes the Law of Mind to re-adjust the disturbed subconscious patterns in the patient, and a healing results.

The practitioner affirms that God in the patient is in action as health. He then denies each symptom and its mental cause and affirms the opposite or the positive. The Law of Mind accepts his conviction and acts upon it and makes the healing a reality. Anyone can do this. It requires a knowledge of the technique and a practice of it, but it requires nothing else. God is not interested in the academic background of the person using his principles. The electric light is not interested in whose home it shines. It is neither conscious of garret or of palace. It knows only how to shine. God can be only God. Health is the result of an orderly and balanced arrangement of patterns in the subconscious, and anyone who can spiritually recondition his thinking through this technique can heal. The simple and the great can do it. The intellectual and the unlearned can do it. Life responds to a recognition of Itself. It does not sit in judgement on the person who recognizes its divinity. It gives to all alike. The infinite Mind is everywhere evenly present and the whole of It is available to you or to anyone else. It has no favorites, It knows no religions.

The Bible teaches healing through a spiritual and psychological technique. Both the Old and New Testaments have within them the instruction that as the sins (the negatives) of a person are released his health automatically appears. When his deep inner fears, hurts and guilt feelings are faced and then denied, the mental pathway is open to the affirmation of health and the person improves. Religion has been a health factor in the history of men because it has forgiven his sins, thereby to some extent releasing the negative pressures of the subconscious. Despite this, religion has not realized that such negatives are the cause of bodily disease. Most of the sins, the negatives, which the churches forgave were ones dealing with morality. The psychological causes of disease are not always immoral ones, they may be as simple as deep seated fears, hostility, and other neurotic symptoms. These the churches have not attempted to heal.

In modern metaphysics the whole area of the subconscious and the negatives therein are spiritually denied and thereby cast out. Morality is left to the good sense of the individual functioning in today's culture, and he is not constantly warned that "the wages of sin is death" (Romans 6:23). He is shown that any negative emotion is unhealthy and should be faced and cleared if he wants to remain a healthy person. Many people have remained moral in their ways of living, yet their subconscious minds have been polluted with other negatives which they could have and still retain their position as respectable citizens in their community. In this new technique a spiritual catharsis of the subconscious is made and healing results.

Spiritual mind healing is not based on the premise that Jesus healed but on the premise that there is a law of healing. It is a technique which works, and Jesus intuitively used it, while you can use it with a full conscious knowledge of the way it works. Healing is a mental science and Jesus demonstrated it, but did not originate it. There are records of healing in the Old Testament times. Both the prophets, Elijah and Elisha did great amounts of healing. Other ancient religious histories give accounts of healings. Jesus was the first man who knew what he was doing when he did it. He healed with understanding, for he said that a corrected belief would produce a corrected situation. In our language today we would say that he intuitively realized that unhealthy patterns in the subconscious made man sick and as these were forgiven and rechannelled the man became whole again.

You will never be convinced of spiritual mind healing until you have healed yourself or someone dear to you. The general public has no acceptance of spiritual healing and wants none. Its reliance on the medical profession is complete and its needs in general are met through medical practice. But, if you have the courage to stand on the spiritual principle that God is all in all, and can understand yourself as an unlimited action of the one perfect Mind, you can heal yourself and others and be convinced of the Truth. Take one physical problem and go to work on it.

Here are some simple rules to follow. Make audible statements defining the nature of God. Six or eight simple statements are enough. Next, make audible statements defining yourself as a spiritual expression of life. Be certain to stress the fact in these that as Life is unconditioned so you are unconditioned. Then make several strong denials of the condition, naming the problem frankly, and follow these with four or six affirmative statements of the fact that God knows no disease, no imperfection and therefore, in God's knowledge of you only health exists and operates. In closing your treatment get a sense of conviction that what you have said is true and know that your subconscious mind accepts the treatment. Do this not more than twice each day and between treatments keep your mind off the problem. Naturally, the more you do this type of healing, the more certain you are and the more accurate you are in technique.

Always remember that the healing is done by your clearance of negative patterns in the subjective, so that the already existing perfect patterns which are eternally within you are given freedom to act. Your human mind cannot heal your body. You do not know

how to grow a hair on your head, a fingernail, nor
how to heal a simple burn on your arm. The infinite
Spirit in you is the Knower of these things. As you
admit your human ignorance and affirm your divine
Knowing, whatever needs to be done is done in perfect
order. While you are sick the power of God is trying
to make you well. Your treatment lets God do what
His Mind wants to do.

Your treatment brings to an end the conflict in the
valley of decision. It calls a halt to the battle of
Armageddon, the battle in your subconscious between
the positive and negative patterns. It brings that peace
which passes human understanding for it is based on
divine understanding of yourself as the beloved outlet
of the eternal Mind. Respect the God of the ages with
its prophets and messiahs. But, only the God of the
moment can heal and in the God of the present you are
immersed. What God has been is historical and theological speculation, but what God is now you can
sense with your own mind and feel with your own
emotions. Do this and healing will follow.

For several years in my class instruction to train
practitioners in New York City's First Church of Religious Science, I have given the students the following
treatment. They have used it regularly, and the results
in actual cases have been many. I offer it to the readers
of this book:

There is one Presence, one Power, one Mind and one Law—God. I am the individualization of God and I express God fully.

In my subconscious mind is the pattern of my body at its peak of perfection.

I now declare that this treatment is the word of God. It is the two-edged sword which goes into my subconscious at this instant, uncovering and revealing this original perfect pattern of body. This treatment, being the word of God, now destroys all other body patterns and all false beliefs which may have been added or attached to this perfect pattern.

This Divine pattern of body is now re-activated (resurrected) by the spirit and is now manifested in outer expression.

It is the only pattern of body which operates in me and my outer body becomes like it. This the Law of Mind does.

I rejoice in this perfect body and give thanks for it. This is the Truth right here and right now. Amen.

8

---•◆•---

Your Mind Is Your Future

ONE OF THE indications that we are in a sick society today is the fact that too few people look ahead with great expectations. It is now apparently normal to view the future as uncertain, insecure and possibly treacherous. The years to come are dreaded by many and the present day emphasis on the problems of old age contributes to a steady decline of vision and hope. People now are considered past their prime at forty-five and are almost unemployable after the age of fifty. Youth and education have taken the spotlight and money has become the stage upon which we play.

Spiritual values have been relegated to the sidelines by the masses of people. Church attendance in most cases is either from habit or to appear respectable in the community. To reach the age of sixty-five and retire on a pension supplemented with Social Security is the only future for many people. This tragic acceptance of defeat is a race belief with power that has to be met in your consciousness.

The teaching that the future can be good, that age is the accumulation of wisdom and efficiency and that no door is ever fully shut has been in the spiritual thinking of the ages. Every religion has proclaimed it and every Messiah has preached it. The Bible states that you can have a good future if you handle your present life rightly. The metaphysical understanding of God as the action of mind and life in man, will lift you out of the pessimism of the race belief and show you that your future is dependent upon your knowledge of God, not on what masses of people have accepted as true.

You are in an unlimited universe. It is conditioned in your experience only by your concept of it. Your subjective acceptance of either good or bad in the world in which you live causes it to react that way. Your expectation of your world is actually your expectation of yourself. You can see only effect like unto cause. What you believe to be true of yourself becomes a law of action to your world. Whether your future is great with glory or inhibited with disease and lack, the universe remains the same. The screen upon which the movie is shown is forever untouched by the showing. It knows not whether the picture is a constructive or destructive one. It remains forever itself. Life allows you to think as you please, but it always produces for you what you think.

Jesus was an optimist in the finest sense of that word. He expected people to live in peace, to love greatly and to prosper. He taught that life responded to you according to your beliefs. He healed the incurable and prospered the destitute. He would never have done this if he believed that life could not be richer and finer with each passing year. Today, we expect the incurable to die and we offer only enough aid to the destitute to keep them alive in their destitution. It does not enter the mind of the average man that spiritual understanding can change any situation for the better. That it can do so has been proven by thousands of the readers of this book.

It is spiritually essential to keep your vision of the future positive no matter what others say or believe. On every side you are beset with the "signs of the times." You are reminded of your frailty, your limitations and the fact that the world is becoming increasingly more complicated and less sure. People who have a knowledge of the omnipresent action of God cannot accept these material verdicts as either true or possible. You have to take your stand one way or the other. You have to serve God or mammon. A divided mind is unstable and never produces a creative idea. Jesus said that a house divided, would always fall. He was describing your consciousness when you say you believe in God and at the same time believe that the future is conditioned and rather hopeless.

A member of my congregation taught me a good lesson. Ten years ago she came to me with her problems. They were very serious problems and I did my best to give her a new viewpoint about them. I knew she was a person of wealth and some of her problems dealt with the cost of living on the scale to which she was accustomed. She told me she was sixty-seven years old. I casually said, "Why not use your money as you please. After all your life expectancy is only another ten or fifteen years." She told me very firmly and definitely that she was going to live to be ninety and go dancing any night she pleased until that age. Today, at seventy-seven she is dancing as much as she ever did. Her body has resiliency, no indication of disease and her mind is still planning what she will do in the next ten years. You might say this is an exceptional case. It is not. This woman enjoys living and refuses to believe that "old age" means a quiet dull existence. She creates new situations all the time and wears out many of us who are a generation younger. She refused to accept defeat. I have never forgotten this and I never again will place an age limitation on anyone.

If you believe in the Mind of God as a ceaseless source of creative ideas, then you cannot indulge in the pessimistic attitude of the world. Every generation has thought it was falling apart and that the end of the world was imminent. They also thought that the youth of their generation were the worst that had ever been. Yet, generation after generation there has been progress. The present is not fraught with danger, and the future will be great for those who have created greatness within themselves. God still leaves man free. The Infinite cannot inhibit Its own creation, but Its creation can easily limit itself by believing in a portentous pathway ahead.

You look at your future through your present problems. Your consciousness knows these problems and is colored by them. The future is not conditioned, but your consciousness is. Through this science, you can clear your consciousness and have a larger and better view ahead. Unhappy, you see the future as an endless round of disappointment. Joyous, you look ahead to triumphs. Your thinking determines what shall be. Knowing this, you can predicate what you want by thinking of it as a present reality. Say to yourself:

I live in the presence of the infinite Mind, which is God. In this presence there is no limitation. It knows no age, no circumstance nor condition. I am not bound by the race acceptance of defeat. I am an individualized expression of Life. I now affirm that my future is one of progress, creative activity and financial security. This is not dependent upon world conditions. It is dependent upon my consciousness and I know God as my

present experience and as my future one. I fear
nothing, for my faith in the one Mind is great.
This is the Truth and my subconscious mind ac-
cepts this Truth and proceeds to bring to pass
conditions which are in accord with it.

You may ask, "What is going to happen to me in
the next ten years?" Remember one thing, nothing can
happen to you unless it happens through you. Your
consciousness is the sieve, through which your experiences pass from idea to form. No one has any way of
knowing what the next ten years will bring, but those
who live from the higher viewpoints of life have little
to fear. God always takes care of those who take care
of their own states of mind and keep them on the
constructive side of life. Mind upholds Its creation,
when Its creation acts according to the principles of
Mind. Most people in fearing the future are like a
man rowing a boat upstream. It is the hardest pathway
to follow. Its detours take you through fears, suspicions, distrust and despair.

Those who walk this way are in darkness. They cry
out for the light, asking for it to come upon them from
without. Yet, within them is that Presence which says
"Follow thou me." From within is the light of mind
that leads to security. Accumulate what you will, use
every material guarantee you can invent, but the future
is not in these. It is in your mind and heart. The right-

minded move forward under an inner impulsion of security. The fearing bog down in the speculations of evil. The wise have always said that man stands at the fork in the road. He chooses his way and the result is like unto his choice.

Which road to take? You will unconsciously select the one which is in accord with the sum total of your subconscious patterns, beliefs and acceptances. A few minutes each day contemplating the higher facets of Life will steer you aright. The Infinite guides those who know Its action and to know this action you have to think in its terms. These terms are large, grand and magnificent. The petty thinker does not grasp them for his interest is only in where he is, not where he may be going. He looks down, not up. He faces facts rather than conceiving great and larger ideas. He says he is a realist when he needs to be an idealist. "I will lift up mine eyes unto the hills, from whence cometh my help." (Psalm 121:1)

There is no plan in the universal creative Mind for evil. There is only a long range plan for good. "And God saw everything that he had made, and, behold, it was very good." (Genesis 1:31) This Mind is still gazing at the manifest universe, Its own body of expression and knowing its goodness. It is always knowing you as a part of Its self-conscious goodness. Like the children of Israel you need to fight the Philistines in order to have a future that is good. These inner negative states are your only enemies and the only power they have to win over you is the power you give them through your thinking upon them.

The children of Israel represent the God-guided man. Each time they forsook their spiritual guidance they were placed in bondage to another nation. In each time of bondage a prophet appeared and told them that their land would be restored to them if they returned to the worship of the one true God. Often they did this and their land was returned. Each prophet proclaimed that their future was in their own hands. Forsake the God of their fathers and they would perish; be faithful unto Him and no evil would be on their pathway. This symbol cannot be improved upon for history bears witness to the facts.

Mentally deny your fears out of existence. They have enslaved you too long. As the Israelites drove the Philistines from their land, so you can drive out of your subconscious mind those beliefs which fasten you in pessimism. The universe will not fail you, the law of Mind will produce for you your good, and God is going to be God for evermore. But to clear consciousness is not as simple as it seems. It means definite work every hour of the day. There is no quick easy way to the spiritual development necessary to be certain of good ahead. Every time any kind of a negative begins in your thinking, cut it in half. Don't let a full negative sentence complete itself. Affirm constantly that your mind is spiritually energized and only the good that you want is true. Hour after hour, day after day this has to be done. In the beginning stages you will weary of it. You will feel that it is not getting you anywhere. But, this steadfast discipline is necessary.

For years you have thought anything you chose to think. You have worried for days, you have feared for many hours. You let your mind run riot as it chose. Now, you are taking control. You are digging new channels, forming new mental habits and giving creative order to your emotions. It takes time, but the results are certain. It is mental housecleaning plus refurnishing. You are throwing out the patterns of failure and doom and replacing them with patterns of security and faith. You are destroying evil, and at the same time glorifying God. You are providing the kind of mind that the Infinite can use for the production of a greater good. You are becoming a vehicle through which Ideas of greatness can function.

This dispels the inner darkness and lets the Light shine through. It does not require church attendance, although church attendance will help the process, provided it is a metaphysical church. It requires no further study but further study of books similar to this one will encourage you on the pathway. Life only asks that you think in Its terms, love in Its way and plan ahead a larger and greater experience than you have ever had before.

The world does not believe that the future is un-conditioned, so the average man has a conditioned future. He expects trouble and experiences trouble. He expects the disadvantages and ailments of old age, and has them. He sits back and says that these are to be expected, that they are natural.

Fortunately, these false conclusions are not true, and in each generation there are mentally alert people who prove their falsity. You can be one of these people. Start right now to think and act as though the years ahead will be better than any you have yet known. Be a prophet to this generation. Give evidence that you really want the years of your life to be full and in-teresting, and then be certain you are an interesting person.

I talk with lonely people a great deal. They come to my lectures and to my office. They are usually drab people. Their clothes may be smart, but their attitude of defeat and isolation is evident. They are not bitter but they are unhappy. Often as I listen to their con-versation I think "Would I like to spend an evening with this person?" In almost all cases, I would not. Why? Because they have somewhere never developed the inward capacity of being a creative, interesting person. The psychological reasons for this are many and their plight is understandable from that view-point.

A drab future indicates a spiritual lassitude. It indicates that the well of interest in life has dried up. There is a great deal of help for the lonely if the Spirit in them can be stimulated in some way; if they can find ways to make their consciousness alert to vital ideas and thus be an interesting person. Have you ever considered what kind of a guest you really are when you visit friends? Is your run of the mill conversation such that it is contributing something interesting to the other people? Here is a treatment that will be of help if this is one of your problems:

I am a part of all that is. There is no isolationism in Life, for Life is the action of God. I am a vital, creative center of intelligence, love and graciousness. No more loneliness, for Divine Love in me pours Itself forth through me to all people. This Love in action through me causes a loving response in all people. I now draw to myself those who are like-minded. I am a giving, a receiving consciousness in the Mind and Love of God. I rejoice in people, and I find the good that is in them. I am not unconsciously afraid of others. I know that the Spirit in all people is warm, friendly and loving. I give thanks for all whom I know, and for all whom I shall meet.

Condition yourself with the attitude of any idea and that idea will manifest for you. Condition yourself with the idea of Love and you will have loving people in your world. Condition yourself with creative interests and you will be wanted and invited. The future can be filled with wonderful people when your consciousness is prepared to experience them. While loneliness affects all age levels, it becomes an increasing fear as the latter years are surveyed. Immediate spiritual action on your part right now will make certain the pleasantness of your later years.

You may say that your problem is not one of loneliness, but you fear the future because you see no way to have sufficient money in the years to come. Start right now, this very day, to change your patterns on income and disbursements. Money is one of the ways in which God circulates in your life. It is not limited to certain age levels. Despite all the material statistics you may be able to gather you cannot convince me that a sincere, clear pattern on money and income will fade away merely because the calendar moves ahead. Start today affirming that in all the years to come you will be a consistent receiver and distributor of money. Affirm that all money belongs to the Infinite, and that you have every right to your share, and your share is determined by your money pattern in the subconscious mind. If you believe that you have to work to get money, then know that you will always be doing some creative work for which you receive a large income. Don't wait until you have been retired on a pension to do this. Now is the appointed time.

Growth of spiritual consciousness is a gradual thing. It usually takes place without your being aware of it, because it is a subconscious action. It is the gradual production by your conscious thinking and treating of larger patterns of good. If each year you live with less fear and more faith, you are growing in the ways of the Spirit. You need have no fear. Each time that fear of lack, fear of disease or fear of being alone enters your mind, clear it out and affirm the action of God as its opposite.

The acorn slowly but surely brings forth the oak tree. Just as surely does spiritual thinking produce security and peace of mind. You evolve gradually but you evolve. Place no blame on person, situation or the national economy. Examine yourself and see what your future will be. It will be your present mind extended. Think what you want in your tomorrow while you are busy today. The future is always now. "Beloved, now are we the sons of God." (I John 3:2)

You cannot put a mortgage on the future which the Mind of God has planned for you. But, you can put a mortgage of fear and negative expectation on your own subconscious mind, and prevent the future from being a happy, prosperous and creative one. The growing mind does not age, and its growing consciousness maintains health in the body and money in the pocket. But the consciousness that shrivels with fear causes the body to diminish in vigor and the high cost of living to become a major point of attention.

The problems you have to meet each day are sufficient to use all your mental and emotional energy. To have in addition a constant over-all problem of fear of the future, inhibits your ability to meet today with ease. God has never yet made a man worry. God has never yet made a man to fear. The beneficent Presence and the all-knowing Mind has created all things and given to them the ability to grow and become fulfilled. This Presence bids you acknowledge Its gifts of mind, body, friends, good work and freedom in money. Rejoice in these as God's actions for you and they will never grow less. The appreciative mind moves forward in security.

Your destiny is greatness. Emerge from the consciousness which gropes in the dark for bits and pieces and behold the Light within you. "That was the true Light, which lighteth every man that cometh into the world." (John 1:9) You are the unconquerable expression of Life as long as you do not bog down in the race patterns of fear, old age and illness. The way ahead, whether you are twenty or seventy, is in your hands. God gives you the tools, but you must do the work.

9

The Necessity of Flexibility

YOU ARE A PART of the cosmic process. In the last
hundred years man has taken on a new understanding
of himself. Formerly he thought of himself as a part
of the life on this earth, but now he perceives that the
cosmos is his home and the limitations of time and
space are lessening all the time. He realizes that he has
to think in larger terms and accept himself in a larger
framework. He invents man-made satellites to circle
the earth as exploring stations for greater discoveries
in space. He knows that the nearest constellations one
day will be contacted. So, the earth becomes to man
merely a base of operations in a larger picture.

Man sees himself in great perspectives. These do not
inflate the ego, they stimulate the true humility of his
spiritual self. He is beginning to know what the spiritually Wise have always known, that infinity is man's
home and eternity is man's time. What your grand-
father would have considered a flight of fancy, you

consider an actual possibility. The man on the street
is no longer awed by astronomical assumptions. He
accepts them and broadens his horizon to fit this larger
scene.

To live in this larger area of the cosmos, you have
to enlarge your thinking to encompass such tremendous ideas. Ideas not only of extended space and possibly extended explorations, but ideas that will enable
you to live with creative activity in this larger scene.
The man who lived to eat, sleep and make money is
lost in this new concept. These minor goals are as
nothing when the mind begins to function in infinity
and eternity. The cosmic explorations require a greater
man than the one whose sole aim is material security
during a life span of seventy to eighty years.

You can be this new man at home in the cosmos
provided you are mentally and emotionally flexible
enough to live from a larger premise. It means the en-
larging of your perspectives of security. It moves security from things to ideas. In the past three genera-
tions we have seen the gradual acceptance of the idea
that there is nothing impossible on the face of the
earth. Now we enlarge this understanding to realize
that there is nothing impossible in the cosmic order.
Invention, research and progress have made us aware
that we are still on the threshold of all that the Infinite
Mind has conceived for us to have, to experience and
to enjoy. "Eye hath not seen, nor ear heard, neither

have entered into the heart of man, the things which God hath prepared for them that love him." (I Corinthians 2:9)

You are the universal man. To you is given more than has ever been given to anyone on the face of this globe. In no other time have so many facts, so much ease and so many possibilities been available to everyone. There is a greater knowledge of the ways in which the Divine manifests and of your place in this creative process. This all necessitates responsibility on your part. It demands that you arise from the petty states of personal viewpoints and join the saints, saviours and scientists who see the grand outworking of a larger Mind in Its unconditioned cosmos.

This requires flexibility on your part. The adjustment from the little world to the infinite order is not easy to make. But, make this change you must if you want the benefits of that which will be. God's man lives in the consciousness of that which will be. Material man lives in the contentment of that which is. The latter is born, accomplishes little and dies a respectable death. Nothing remains of him save an expensive tombstone and the permanent records of his birth and death in the local city hall archives. This man is of no account. He has been a receiver of life but not a giver. He has taken from his generation all that he could get, but he has failed to contribute anything lasting. Even the financial inheritance he bequeaths is fought over and used with glee by his relatives.

What kind of man does fit the New Order? One who is willing to constantly change, who is able to let go of the past and the present to embrace the future, and who is flexible enough to realize that all things that now are will pass away and new things will appear in perfect order and in right sequence. The man who believes in the Infinite Mind and Its eternal processes of unfoldment, forever creating, releasing and recreating the universe; the man who can dare to be free in things and in personal relationships; the man who can say both yes and no with ease and without guilt; that is the man who is worthy of the New Order at hand. "No man, having put his hand to the plough, and looking back, is fit for the kingdom of God." (Luke 9:62)

You will need more flexibility in the next fifty years than you have ever before needed. To remain rigid in the coming expansion will mean disintegration, stagnation, infection and a living death. The open mind, the changing consciousness and the welcoming heart are the signs of the man who will live with joy in an ever progressively improving cosmos. The Infinite Mind will act in this man, and the Infinite Love will maintain him in wholeness and contentment. His shifting environment will not confuse him, for more of heaven will appear with each change. Can you make the mental adjustments necessary to live in this larger order?

Is your thinking up to date? Are your values based on current conditions, or are you using yesterday as the yardstick for today? Jesus looked ahead and measured his world by the standard of that which would be. He envisioned a perfect world. So do the scientists and the metaphysicians today. It can logically and scientifically be planned out on paper how to bring about this perfect world. The only thing which stands in the way of this heaven on earth is humanity not knowing its divinity. Everyone realizes the futility and nonsense of war, but each of us carries his little hates and jealousies. We expect the nations to live in peace, when we, as individuals, cannot.

If the minds of men could be spiritually stimulated to accept change as it comes and welcome the improvements that come with it, the heaven foretold of old could be a reality. You are the starting point for this spiritual revolution to bring about a better world in an infinite cosmos of which you are a part. To date the scientists have been unable to find people on other planets. So, we can assume that present man is the probable only outlet of self-consciousness, the only means God has for consciously creating new and better conditions.

Your mind is the place to be flexible. Calisthenics

may keep your body flexible, but the body is not the creative phase of your being. Your consciousness was created to be an inlet process and outlet of mind action. Memory was created for the purpose of retaining information that would be of help in your mental processes. Instead, through the ages man has stored in his subconscious the race patterns plus his own set opinions. These are your enemies. These are the trouble spots of consciousness. This is why every religious system has had a technique for cleansing man's consciousness.

The lives of all great spiritual souls show the methods they used to erase the subconscious beliefs that the world opinion has power. No man has ever achieved spiritual greatness until he has met this in some way within himself. Some have renounced the world and lived in solitude. Others have done all kinds of penance. In this science we do neither. We see the race beliefs as the power of evil, and we destroy them out of our subconscious minds through treatment.

The race mind believes that the world is a place where we must struggle from birth to death with the problem of evil. It believes that sickness is natural, death is certain and pain is to be expected. It believes that the only material security there can be is money and more money. It believes that man has to struggle for a living. It believes that few people can be trusted, and that love is primarily a sex function. The race belief expects trouble all through life and hopes for eventual peace of mind in a future heaven granted by a distant deity.

If you will examine your former opinions, you may be surprised how much of the above you have unconsciously accepted without thinking. Watch your friends and see if they are not impelled by just such basic conclusions about life. These unconscious negatives have been the greatest single stumbling block to the progress of man. If you are to live in a larger understanding of life, these have to be negated whenever they appear in your thinking. As they are deeply embedded in your thinking, they are not easily destroyed. Many of them you unconsciously accepted as a child. Others you accepted without question as they were a part of everyone's thinking and conversation. Spiritual efficiency and creative living demands that you expel them from your life for all time.

As a good starting point on your endless meeting of these old race opinions, you can treat yourself this way:

God, the one mind, rules and governs all. This infinite Mind is all cause, all power and all truth. The Intelligence of God is mine, and my consciousness is the seat of Its operation. I am a spiritual being and my consciousness is an activity in the Mind of God. Therefore, I now deny out of my subconscious mind every negative race belief. I am Spirit and therefore, I am not subject to disease, death, unhappiness, lack or frustration. These no longer exist in my subconscious mind. I do not have to labor nor do I have to expect a defeated old age. These I reject once and for all. My consciousness is God's consciousness and I am not subject to the opinions of the world. I am subject to Truth and to Truth alone. I affirm my permanent health, happiness and creative self-expression. I affirm my faith in the good. I affirm that Life lives through me in ever new and better ways. I am a growing, evolving, expanding expression of the life and mind of God. I subconsciously accept this treatment, and it is done.

Having taken such action you have made your mind more flexible. It is more liable to attract creative ideas with which you can increase the distance to the horizon of your experience. We all live in too small worlds. It is too easy to be comfortable in the routines of work, home, friends and the same usual situations. Only so far as you are uncomfortable are you growing in mind. The contented have never improved the world nor helped the lot of their fellowman. They have remained in the uncreative routines of the usual and their sole efforts were to make certain that no person nor condition would upset their minor happiness. They missed the one great happiness of being, the happiness of daring and courage.

There is a divine discontent. It is the most normal condition that can happen to you. If you do not have it, it indicates you are bound in the lethargy of false contentment based on an untrue idea of security. Without this inner gnawing toward greatness you are as chaff that is of no value. With it, you have all that is needed to become the man for the larger cosmic order. Only the forward-looking man with a discontent of things as they are is capable of creating a new heaven and a new earth. Never be satisfied with the present, for this impedes the birth pangs of that which will be. It prevents the new from having conception in your thinking.

There are no finalities. Everything is changeable. Everything is flexible. In a time of despair you may think that you never again can be happy, healthy or at peace. But, that is merely the negative of depression holding sway in your subconscious. It is a temporary signing away of your spiritual authority to the devil, the race negatives. When the depression has passed, you again see clearly. Never mortgage your future by making final statements. The person who says, "I never will be happy again," or some similar statement is speaking a finality that is false. The spiritual Mind knows no such facts or fancies. God is a progressive, ever-changing action in the consciousness of man.

God in you is the intuitive knowing that nothing is final, and all things and situations pass away in order that greater experiences shall be born. The doors of the kingdom of heaven are never shut. Divine Ideas forever flood the consciousness of man. They are the impelling force for greatness. They offer the flexible consciousness, the eternal adventure of the new, the fresh and the different. They are heeded only by those who know the Truth of their own being. Those who know that they are the inlet and the outlet of Ideas born of a larger Mind and a greater Love become the vehicles of the Spirit. Inflexibility breeds decay of creative mind action. It is the most vicious problem facing you.

The greater man to experience a greater cosmic order will be a loving man. He will be large enough in his understanding of God and of man to know that love is life's most important essential. He will be required to give up the pettiness of personal possessiveness. He will love with intensity a few, but he will love with definiteness all whom he knows. He will know that you cannot hate, dislike, misjudge nor be jealous and be a creative part of the full order of life. He will handle personal relationships with skill. This skill will not be a psychological one for that is only the human mind trying to behave itself. He will handle them with a skill born of his sure knowing that spiritually he is one with everyone and he cannot afford to let anything disrupt this unity of the spirit.

The reason that Jesus could love so completely was his awareness that he was a part of all life, all mind and all love. He knew that the divine idea of Love was omnipresent in all and through all. He sought this Love where others sought personal gain. He never possessed anyone, was never jealous of anyone. He knew that within him was the divine Incarnation and he needed not to compete with anyone. You need never compete, when you know yourself as God knows you. To compete indicates that you do not yet know your true spiritual nature. You still believe others more important. You still worship at the altars of prestige and power. All men are equal in the mind of God, and all have the same spiritual potentials. Once you have convinced your subconscious of this you are free of all competition.

What your fellowman accomplishes is none of your business. He may be far more successful materially than you, but that is not the goal of living. He may do the right things and know the right people who are required for today's false image of success. All this means little to him whose knowledge of the love of God is large. He is too occupied in keeping his peace with himself and with his family and co-workers to bother with an untrue picture of life. God loves by means of you. All the Love there is focalizes in your emotions seeking a balanced outlet. It gives without price. It is the greatest single ingredient in living flexibly. It takes away all the competitive stresses. It unites on a solid foundation those who know It aright. It makes no claims and has no ownership. Its sole purpose is to give, and it cares not whether it receives in like measure or not.

It is no wonder that both Jesus and the writer John made Love the key point in Christianity. The Old Testament had emphasized the law, but Jesus knew that the law without love was a wrong premise. Only as law was complemented by love could the full man emerge in flexibility. Rigidity of thinking can not take place when a deep sense of love is a power at the subconscious level. A good treatment to make subjective love effective is:

I am ready to let Love be in me and through me as a flexible power of good. I now release all hatred, unpleasantness and jealousy. God in the midst of me is right action and loving action. There is no competitive belief. I am equal to all, and all are equal to me. I understand the Christ in every man, and the Christ in me is loved by every man. There are no more misunderstandings, for love rules and governs my subconscious mind. I live in a cosmic universe and I cannot hate any-

one, any nation or any race. I love with the love
of God. I am unified within myself, and I see all
people as phases of myself. For this, I give thanks
and am glad.

To remain flexible you have to watch your reactions toward both the past and the future. These are
the two subconscious trouble spots in human thinking.
If the traditions or negatives of the past govern your
decisions regarding new ideas, you will find the old
patterns or rigidity dominating. No matter how great
or how good a past tradition or wisdom may be, there
is always a better one for this day. The worship of the
old, the past and the former have enthralled millions
and prevented their progress from taking place at the
rate it should have progressed. One would think that
God went out of business two thousand years ago, that
Truth would never be revealed again and that man
would never capture a new idea from the infinite
Mind.

Every moment of every day you are in the Divine
Intelligence which is revealing the ideas necessary for
that moment. The ideas that are right for this time
appear in this time. They will not fit the ways of the
past, for they are devised to bring to pass something
greater than the past. People keep up to date in clothing
fashions, but they premise their thinking on patterns a
generation or more out of date. Streamline your mind,

modernize your thinking and pour out love to as many people as possible. Watch constantly that you are not biased by tradition. A thing is good only if it is good right here and right now. It was good in its own time and place, but we carry too much excess baggage subconsciously. Glenn Clark once wrote, "If you want to travel far and travel fast, travel light." *

Ancient wisdom may or may not be followed as a guide. There is sufficient good modern spiritual thinking to take care of your needs. I shall never know why religions do not become as outmoded as other systems, but their holiness cannot be questioned without raising a storm of condemnation. The public wants the old with its symbols and rituals. There is less inflexibility in man's religious acceptance than in any other area of his life. When it comes to his church he is rigid, dogmatic and final. Yet, if you question him as to why he believes that particular way, you will find his answers to be trite and not at all convincing. God is revealing Himself in every generation and in new ways to meet the needs of that generation. Today, the teaching of God as infinite Mind operating through a Law is the truth for this generation, but only those who are free will adopt it.

It is a spiritual and psychological challenge to remain flexible. Fortunately these modern times offer you more variety of ideas, things and situations than

* *The Thought Farthest Out,* Macalester Park Publishing Co.

any generation ever has had at its command. You cannot blame anyone but yourself if you do not make steady progress in the unfolding of your consciousness. A daily checkup on your ways of thinking and feeling will show you where you are. Say yes to all that intrigues you, inspires you and helps you grow. Make a definite effort to get the ideas you want. Search them out and follow through on them. Find the people who think as you do and have fellowship with them. Old friends may have to take second place to new ones, but this is right.

Be liberal, progressive and venturous and the larger scene will unfold with greater good than you have ever known before. Think of God in the grandest terms possible. Think of your own spiritual nature in equally large terms. Fasten your attention on your possibilities and how to attain them. Know that the Infinite welcomes the person who can move forward, investigate the new and release that which has served its purpose. This is the flexibility of the Spirit. It is your flexibility now.

10

The Technique of Demonstration

WE LIVE IN GLASS mental houses. Consciousness determines experience, and experience denotes consciousness. Too many people have verbally agreed to principles like the ones expressed in this book, but you would never know their spiritual beliefs from watching their experience. The ideas and their presentation satisfy their intellect, but they never give these ideas the emotional acceptance necessary for them to become subconscious patterns of action. Jesus said that his listeners could be divided into two types, the hearers and the doers. Modern metaphysical churches have both groups in their congregations despite the fact that our science is one of action, production and result. This is not at all alarming for the greater number do demonstrate these truths and their lives give evidence that is convincing.

What is a demonstration? It is a tangible result of a constructive change of consciousness on a spiritual premise. It is one which would not happen under normal conditions nor through normal channels. Metaphysicians expect the impossible and the unusual to happen. When told of a phenomenal recovery of health they are not excited, because it is normal to the right-thinking person to have such a result. When a business man describes an unusual change in his field which has benefited him, a change which would not normally take place, it is a demonstration.

You have a right to expect results from your spiritual thinking. Your spiritual thinking changes you. It doesn't change the world. It doesn't change other people. It changes you, and that is all that needs to be changed. Once you have changed, the results of this change appear in your circumstances. Others will see that your knowledge of God and your right understanding of yourself as the action of God, bring to pass definite improvements.

The mind of God awaits your recognition, and the power of God awaits your direction. You need neither repentance nor salvation to make your demonstration. You do need decision, acceptance and continued right thinking. You need to take a definite stand and then not waver from the premise that the action of Mind is bringing to fruition your idea. It takes mental stamina to practice metaphysics. This Science is not for the half-hearted. It demands the full attention and use of the mind and emotions. There is no place for discouragement in this practice.

Your goal must be clear and you must want what you want with ardor, vitality and authority. There is no place in spiritual understanding for wishful thinking. The infinite Mind acts with an exactness, and wishful thinking can produce only vaporous nothings. The seed planted in consciousness must by the Law of mind bring forth after its own kind. Sweetness and light produce little of any value. They are a dodge, an escape and a delusion. Beware of people who are always sweet and kind. There is something being covered up in the unpleasant depths of their subconscious. That is why piety must be overcome before any attempt is made to practice spiritual mind techniques.

A scientific treatment is actually a battle of the wits in the consciousness of the one treating. It is making fear unreal and all doubts to flee. It is mental argument to arrive at the complete conclusion that what you want exists in the now for you and will appear at once through spiritual action on the part of the universal subconscious mind. You wrestle with your own states of consciousness with the same agility and ability that professional wrestlers have to have in their bodies. "For we wrestle not against flesh and blood, but against principalities, against powers, against the rulers of the darkness of this world." (Ephesians 6:12)

The principalities of mind are your negative certainties. The rulers of darkness are your subconscious

the false authority of evil in any of its mani-
s. These must be attacked with strong denials
of their existence. Say to yourself:

*I now direct the living Spirit within me to bring
to pass this demonstration. I know exactly what I
want, and authorize my subconscious mind to act
as a law to make it manifest right now. This treatment is the word of the Spirit and it now destroys
from my subconscious every negative pattern, belief or opinion that is opposite to the thing I want.
The perfect action of the infinite Mind in me now
obliterates all of my self-accepted principalities,
powers and false patterns. I am cleansed of all
unbelief, and the Spirit now has full sway in all
of my consciousness. There is nothing in me to
oppose or delay this demonstration. All channels
are cleared and all doors are opened. Perfect action is now taking place, and what I want, I have.*

The above is a good mental cleansing agent. It should
be spoken aloud with authority daily. It will baptize
your consciousness and give the idea you want demonstrated a clear road to fulfillment. Each time doubt or
fear begins in your thinking, do this treatment right
over again. You may need to speak such words many
times a day in order to allay your suspicions of failure.
If you can keep your consciousness free of your own
negatives, the Law of mind can demonstrate anything.

It's up to you and the mental disciplining you do. On these two factors rests the responsibility for demonstration.

Think of your consciousness as a mental gymnasium in which you prove your strength, develop your spiritual muscles and overcome opponents. The opposite of what you want is the opponent to be destroyed. You are mentally wrestling this false idea and proving your positive spiritual belief to be victorious. Each time you treat yourself, you are gaining over this opposite. You maintain spiritual vigilance to make certain that the negative doesn't slyly attack you when you are off guard. You make certain that you are always in control over the situation. Finally the opponent gives up, and the victory is yours. By your strong denials of the things you don't want they are negated and made ineffective in your subconscious.

The practicing metaphysician works in his mind as a noted scientist works in his laboratory. He knows what to do and knows that the already existing laws of Life will work for him to bring to pass his accomplishment. A treatment doesn't cause something to happen miraculously. A treatment establishes a cause in a Law which produces it. There is no guess work in scientific prayer. There is an exactness as precise as that required to be a chemist or a physicist. The scientist doesn't plead with the laws of his science to accomplish his feats, neither does the metaphysician plead with the

Lord to give him his demonstration. He acts in accordance with the laws of spiritual Science and the result is certain. This point cannot be too strongly emphasized.

To many this technique seems irreligious, but it is not. It is the probable method that Jesus used. The results of using this method in the past hundred years have been so great that they command the respect of any sincere researcher. All manner of sickness has been healed. Every known type of problem has been solved. You may ask if there are any failures. There have been few in comparison with the successes. Like any other science the element of failure is the human element. The manufacturer can produce a perfect automobile, but there is no way of knowing what the driver will do with it. When a person does not make his demonstration, it is difficult to know at what point his consciousness gave more power to the idea he was battling than to the idea he was trying to manifest. Somewhere, though, this happened or there wouldn't have been the failure.

Often it is almost impossible for people to realize that they can have what they want, as long as it is good. They have in their subconscious minds the fixed idea that for some reason God doesn't want them to have the particular form of good they would like. They think of their having it as impossible, so this deep seated pattern affects their facility in using treatment effectively. The orthodox teachings about God are a vicious subconscious limitation, as I mentioned in a previous chapter. This accounts for many of the failures of those using this science. Be certain that you really feel that the Infinite gives without stint to you upon your demand.

"Wherefore take unto you the whole armour of God, that ye may be able to withstand in the evil day, and having done all, to stand." (Ephesians 6:13) To stand in the midst of human adversity and deny the problem and affirm the spiritual pattern of its opposite is not easy, but it has to be done. The withstanding of the evil day is to hold fast to your claim that God is omnipotent and that evil is unreal and cannot endure in the experience of the right-minded man. The whole armour of God is your divine protection when you dedicate your thinking to the answer and not the question, the solution and not the problem. All the affirmative processes of life move into action when a spiritually determined mind declares the Truth.

This Science is not for the timid, it is for the daring. The first fifty years of Christianity were not for the timid. Only brave men and women could take the faith and hold to it. The early Christians braved death, while those who practice this message do not. Yet, it takes spiritual courage to change your mind and keep it changed. The only lions to devour you are your own misconceptions of God and of man, but these are sufficient to make your life drab. Daniel in the lions' den faced them and looked upward. Face your negatives and then lift your consciousness to that Mind in which there is no problem to be solved, no person to be pacified and no debt to be paid. God knows you aright, even though you may not know yourself aright. The universe believes in you, appreciates you and gives its all to you.

Christianity was founded on demonstration not on theology. The followers of Jesus saw the works of his consciousness. They saw disease conquered, hunger fed and debts paid. They believed in him because of the works he wrought. They listened to his teaching of life, but they were more impressed by his actions than by his ideas. The metaphysical movement makes no claim to a correct theology, in fact it has none. It does say to all who will listen that demonstrations are more important than theories. A healed body is more important than the doctrine which may have produced it or may have hindered it. To the chronic worrier a clear freedom from this problem is greater than whether he believes in a trinity or not.

The action of God is instantly available to you. It requires nothing but your recognition of it. The Power is uninterested in your past and the patterns which have caused your present experience. Infinity pervades the finite with Its ever-expanding action of life. It asks no questions and plays no favorites. "Ho, every one

that thirsteth, come ye to the waters, and he that hath
no money; come ye, buy, and eat; yea, come, buy wine
and milk without money and without price." (Isaiah
55:1) You are ever in the midst of the beckoning
Mind which offers Its ideas to you. But you cannot
believe their opposite and demonstrate them. Straight
clear thinking is the road that leads to what you want.
The detours offer themselves with beguiling interest,
but have none of them.

Worry is often pleasant. It is a convenient way of not
having to meet the problem of the instant. By worrying about what may happen, you do not need to act in
the now. It is a delaying action invented by the human
mind to keep the error present. Be sure that you do not
use worry as an escape from demonstrating the Truth.
As the Infinite works neither in the past nor in the
future but in the now, you have to do likewise. Worry
today is trouble tomorrow, and trouble tomorrow is
more cause for worry. It is a vicious circle that en-
snares most people, and yet they know it not.

Above and beyond the human mind is the Divine
Intelligence that knows no evil, thinks no evil and perceives no evil. As you link your mind with this higher
concept your demonstrations appear and your heaven
is at hand. "For as the heavens are higher than the
earth, so are my ways higher than your ways, and my
thoughts than your thoughts." (Isaiah 55:9) To him
who knows this truth, there are no boundaries to his

creative action. Isaiah could stand in the midst of the exiled Jews and say "Look unto Zion," because he knew that if he could get them to think of Jerusalem instead of their exile they would return. Return they did, for his counsel was taken, and as a result the demonstration was made.

Like these people of olden times, look at what you want. Talk in terms of what you want. Consistently believe that what you want is now taking place through the action of the Law of the Spirit. Never admit defeat to another or to yourself. Hold fast to your deep conviction that God honors your thought and acts upon it. Walk mentally around the Jericho of your problem and know the walls will fall. Stand as did Jesus before the cross of your problem and know that it has neither power nor authority. It is nothing but two pieces of wood, and it cannot hurt you, destroy you nor confuse you. Knowing this you are resurrected out of all problems, all unhappiness and all fear.

In you the power of accomplishment is unlimited. But it must have free and open channels through which to work. You alone can clog or clear the channels of consciousness. Blame no one else. You stand at the door of your mind and you determine what goes on within it. To say that others cause your problem is to proclaim your own ignorance. To say that world conditions hold you in bondage is to admit defeat. The universe knows your forward right action, it doesn't know your own unconsciously accepted patterns of defeat. When you know your unconquerable soul, you know what God knows about you.

The power of mind and emotion is the power of God. It is the only power there is, ever has been or ever will be. It is your power now. It requires no special dispensation, nor any particular religious belief. It is given to all for all to use. You can demonstrate through your knowledge of the power of God. You can move the mountains of your own mental inertia. You can have health, happiness, peace of mind and unfrustrated activity. You can have love with all its blessings. To you these are normal and right. If others believe in sickness, poverty, old age and limitation, it is none of your business. Your business is to know God aright and prove in your body and world that the Truth is. All else is unimportant and is not worthy of your attention.

Demonstrate what you want. Don't talk yourself out of your good, and permit no one else to do it either. Here are the basic rules of the scientific way of treating to get what you want.

1. *Affirm your knowledge of God as infinite Mind.*
2. *Select the idea you want to demonstrate. Check this idea to be certain it is good for you and will hurt no one else.*

3. *Make audible statements convincing your own subconscious that this idea is now a fact.*

4. *Deny anything that is opposed to the idea. Deny all fear, all hesitation and all belief that it can't happen.*

5. *Continually think in terms of having the idea already, and that it has appeared as the result of spiritual action.*

6. *Watch your thinking constantly to erase all doubt.*

7. *When the demonstration takes place tell others of the spiritual means you used to bring it to pass.*

All the good you want awaits your recognition and demand upon it. Having done all—stand. Having placed your demand in the subconscious stand firm in your faith and do not waver. You have put on the whole armour of right thinking, and the negatives cannot prevail against your consciousness. You are as an island set in the midst of the ocean of Mind. You are a free agent in an unconditioned power, presence and life. You are the beloved of the infinite Spirit, for through you It reveals all that It is. Stand in this revelation and authorize your experience. Heaven is the normal atmosphere of the man who knows his perfect place in the Divine Plan of being. Come forth from the hells of your mistakes and abide in that pure consciousness of right knowing of Truth.

Be true to the inner man made in the image and likeness of all that Life is. This inner Spirit guides you into greatness. It leads you from the petty to the threshold of the larger scene. It offers the heavenly vista of unexplored possibilities. It bids you remember that you are the son of the living God. Like Jesus, you can say: "To this end was I born, and for this cause came I into the world, that I should bear witness unto the truth. Every one that is of the truth heareth my voice." (St. John 18:37) You need never apologize for your spiritual understanding. It shines as a light unto men. It is healing for those who think rightly. It is a way for those who seek a spiritual technique of life. You are the bearer of glad tidings to your world. Spread them abroad with power and love. Be the person that God intended you to be. This is the victorious attitude of the metaphysician.